Sharing Jesus in a new Millennium

Sharing Jesus in a new Millennium

A practical introduction to evangelism
for Christians everywhere

Rob Frost

Scripture Union

Scripture Union, 207–209 Queensway, Bletchley, MK2 2EB, England.
email: info@scriptureunion.org.uk
Internet:http://www.scripture.org.uk/

First published 2000
ISBN 1 85999 305 2

British Library Cataloguing-in-Publication Data
A catalogue record for this book is available from the British Library.

Cover design by The Five Castles Press Limited.
Cover photograph from the film *Jesus Christ*, distributed by Army of Ants.

Printed and bound in Great Britain by Creative Print and Design (Wales), Ebbw Vale.

CONTENTS

*To all those thousands of Christians
who have dared to Share Jesus
in the UK and in different parts of the world.*

PART I
Principles of Evangelism

Chapter 1

JESUS-CENTRED EVANGELISM

I was twenty-one years of age and had invited a group of friends to join me on a beach mission in the Cornish surf resort of Newquay. It was a daunting experience and I was very nervous. On the second day, however, a very elderly evangelist called Herbert Silverwood arrived unexpectedly.

I was deeply moved that this man, nearly eighty years of age, should come to spend time with me and the team on our first ever beach mission. He was known throughout the country as one of the most outstanding evangelists of his generation. I was even more amazed that he was willing to sleep on the floor in the church vestry! He obviously had an uncomfortable night because at breakfast the next morning he said, 'I had to get up in the night for a rest!'

It was great to have someone around who had been an evangelist for nearly fifty years, and I was constantly pumping him for tips on how to do evangelism well. His advice was simple but profound, and he kept repeating it. 'Tell them about Jesus,' he said. 'If you lift Jesus high, many will be drawn to him.' Day after day I watched Herbert at work on the promenade at Newquay. Every evening hundreds gathered to hear his amazing fund of jokes and hilarious experiences delivered in a broad Yorkshire accent. The holidaymakers loved it, and many stayed on while he went on to tell the familiar stories of Jesus in vivid detail. As he drew a meeting to a close, he would urge his audience to 'follow my Jesus, because he'll do you good!' Afterwards, he would linger to talk to everyone, from kids to octogenarians, from families to teenage hecklers. He never missed an opportunity to talk about Jesus or to speak of his love, yet it was all so spontaneous and natural. It was evident that Jesus was an integral part of Herbert's life.

Sadly, some of the Christians who join me on mission teams each year don't have Herbert's ability to talk about Jesus. They seem to have grown up in a church culture where he is rarely spoken of in a personal way. Some hardly know how to communicate the gospel effectively to people who know nothing about him. But true evangelism will only happen when Christians talk about Jesus in ways that make others want to know him for themselves.

The activity of evangelism has been devalued by many churches who are under the impression that the occasional outreach event, special week of activities or leaflet drop is 'evangelism'. But that may not be what is really happening. They may actually only be advocating the social activities of their local fellowship or promoting their particular denomination. This isn't true evangelism! It is no more than a recruitment drive akin to something which might be undertaken by a golf club or bingo hall. The yardstick for true Christian evangelism is simply this: Are we telling others about our Saviour? Are we really sharing Jesus?

The uniqueness of Jesus

Right from the announcement of his birth, God made it clear that Jesus would be no ordinary man. The nature of his birth marked him out as very different, proclaiming him to be the Son of God and not the son of Joseph. While many people today will accept that Jesus was a great prophet, teacher or healer, they won't accept that he is the Son of God. Yet without appreciating this aspect of his character, they haven't even begun to understand who he is. The early church was so concerned to emphasise this, they made belief in his Sonship their basic confession for baptism. Mark's Gospel underscores its importance by opening with the words, 'The beginning of the gospel of Jesus Christ, the Son of God'.

In the opening years of the new millennium, I believe that the acknowledgement of Jesus as the Son of God is under greater threat than it has been for many centuries. In a multi-cultural and multi-faith society, there is growing pressure to embrace those from other faith communities. We should welcome this kind of dialogue, but there are some tenets of our faith which are non-negotiable, and that Jesus is the Son of God is one of them. This contention over Jesus' identity lies at the very heart of Christian faith, since only when we accept that Jesus is God and truly Divine do we discover who God is and what God is like.

The relevance of Jesus

The task of the evangelist is to tell the story of Jesus, but to tell it in such a way that it relates to the ordinary lives of men, women and children. The challenge is to apply this story in ways that relate to people's search for meaning, and to their deep-rooted and personal felt needs. The longer I do the work of an evangelist, the more amazed I am at just how relevant the Jesus story is. Whatever people are facing, however they are feeling and whoever they are, there is always some aspect of it that can speak directly to them. There are hundreds of 'angles' the evangelist can use to bring the Jesus story to contemporary men and women, but I will list here just a few of them to illustrate my point.

The 'New Age' Jesus

One of the greatest contributions of the Celtic Christians to the richness of our spirituality is that they recognised Christ's immanence in creation and in the whole of life. They grasped the wonder that Christ is not only over all but also in all. His presence pervades the whole of creation and fills every aspect of it. Christ's involvement in creation began right from the very start of time. He is the one who envisioned the changing season, the scudding cloud, the delicate flower, the glowing sunset. He is the one who brought it all into being, who created it all for us to see:

> He is the image of the invisible God, the firstborn over all
> creation. For by him all things were created: things in heaven
> and on earth, visible and invisible, whether thrones or powers
> or rulers or authorities; all things were created by him and for
> him.

In a time of 'New Age' spirituality, the Celtic view of Jesus
may be surprisingly helpful in giving us opportunities to talk
about Jesus in ways with which New Agers will connect. The
New Age thesis that the Divine is immanent in all things can
offer a 'way in' for presenting them with this view of Jesus,
and we can build bridges with them by telling them about the
one whose love infuses the planet.

The powerless Jesus

We live in a world in which many feel powerless and forgotten. But the story of Jesus can bring great strength and comfort to people feeling like this. He was not born in a palace
but a stable. He didn't grow up among kings and princes but
as a refugee in Egypt. He didn't walk the corridors of power
but the road to the cross. He wasn't wealthy or of high social
status; instead he mixed with tax collectors and prostitutes.
This Jesus didn't just get alongside the powerless: he knew
what it was to be marginalised by society.

Not only did Jesus identify with the powerless, he saw his
ministry as one that would bring radical change to their situation, challenging the power structures of the world. At a
synagogue in his home town of Nazareth, he used the words
of the prophet Isaiah to underline this aspect of his mission:

> 'The Spirit of the Lord is on me,
>   because he has anointed me
>   to preach good news to the poor.
> He has sent me to proclaim freedom for the prisoners
>   and recovery of sight for the blind,
> to release the oppressed,
>   to proclaim the year of the Lord's favour.'

All through his earthly ministry Jesus challenged the powerful. The Romans demanded total allegiance to the emperor. The wealthy, land-owning Sadducees demanded allegiance to the status quo. The pious Pharisees demanded allegiance to the observance of ritual. But Jesus wouldn't side with any of them. He refused to support their claims because his priority was the kingdom of heaven, not the kingdoms of the earth. His was a currency that dealt in sacrifice, humility and meekness, which threatened the established power structures, interest groups and political regimes of his day:

> 'You know that the rulers of the Gentiles lord it over them, and their high officials exercise authority over them. Not so with you. Instead, whoever wants to become great among you must be your servant, and whoever wants to be first must be your slave – just as the Son of Man did not come to be served, but to serve, and to give his life as a ransom for many.'

Jesus' own ministry was a demonstration of servanthood. It sometimes overwhelms me that the Lord of all creation came to earth in 'the very nature of a servant'. His life was lived in complete obedience to the will of his Father. This can speak poignantly to those who feel powerless, reassuring them that whatever their circumstances Jesus, the bringer of good news to the poor, is with them just where they are.

The rejected Jesus

Jesus loved the world with a depth of compassion we can't begin to understand. His leap from heaven to earth was made at enormous personal cost and led to painful experiences of rejection.

He was rejected by the people he grew up with, who had known him all his life. Going back Nazareth, back to the carpenter's shop, back to his mother and brothers, and the small close-knit community in which he'd been reared, he might have expected a hero's welcome. Maybe they'd put the flags out for the small-town boy made good. Not a bit of it!

Instead, he met only resistance and murderous hostility.

He was snubbed by the religious elite. When Simon, a Pharisee, invited Jesus to dinner, he didn't invite him to honour him, hear him or affirm him. He offered him none of the marks of hospitality that a Jewish host of the time would have offered his guests – there was no kiss of welcome, no ceremonial washing bowl, no neatly folded towel. Instead, Jesus met with cynicism and mockery. It seems that Simon invited Jesus to humiliate him!

He was rejected by his fellow countrymen. I remember one evening, at sunset, standing on the Mount of Olives, looking down over Jerusalem. It brought alive for me that moment when Jesus looked over that same city and wept:

> 'O Jerusalem, Jerusalem, you who kill the prophets and stone those sent to you, how often I have longed to gather your children together, as a hen gathers her chicks under her wings, but you were not willing.'

Jesus had an aching burden for the people of that great city. He knew their needs and wanted to embrace them with his love. These were not empty sentiments but the expression of one who lived entirely for others and who was feeling deep within himself the pain of their rejection of him.

And finally, he was betrayed and abandoned by his closest friends, the ones whom he might have expected to stick by him through any danger. But when the guards came to arrest him in Gethsemane, they were led there by one of his own disciples and all the others fled in terror, leaving him to face his enemies alone.

Over and over again, the story of Jesus is a story of rejection. He was born in a borrowed stable and buried in a borrowed tomb, and between the two he knew what it was to walk a lonely road. It's little wonder, then, that he was often the friend of the rejected and shrank from no-one. He cared for crooks like Zacchaeus, those of dubious morality like the woman of Samaria, and outcasts like the ten lepers. He still comes alongside life's outcasts today. His story speaks powerfully to anyone who has tasted abandonment and loneliness. His life teaches that through him we can find acceptance, healing and adoption into the family of God.

The Saviour Jesus

Jesus knew what it was to be human – to struggle with temptation, to wrestle with the will of God, to agonise over the cost of total obedience to the Father. He even knew hell, in one bleak moment of separation from God. There was no dark human experience he was not willing to go through as he made his painful pilgrimage to the cross. But as Jesus hung on the cross, taking upon himself the sin of the world, he also became a sacrifice for us. His death is a profound mystery, yet ultimately it became the most momentous event in human history: God taking on our humanity and dying on our behalf. Jesus died that we might know the quality and depth of God's love. He died that he might reach down to where we are and lift us up into the Father's presence. This is the quality of his caring and the magnitude of his compassion. The story of Jesus, then, is a story of hope, a gospel of forgiveness, an opportunity for new beginnings. It is the story of someone who came to rescue us and set us free:

'For God so loved the world that he gave his one and only Son, that whoever believes in him shall not perish but have eternal life. For God did not send his Son into the world to condemn the world, but to save the world through him.'

No longer need we look to the future with despair or fear. No longer need we carry heavy burdens of guilt and failure. We can ask him to save us, to forgive us, and to bring us into the kind of beautiful relationship with God which really makes life worth living.

The risen Jesus

The story of Jesus is a story of personal renewal. Three days after his crucifixion, Jesus came back to life. He overcame sin and suffering; he defeated the power of evil; he broke the hold death has over us. Each of us is invited to share in his victory and to claim it personally. We are invited to live in the joy of his resurrection, no matter what we face. We should know his resurrection power as part of our everyday lives. It should fill us with hope and help us see that whatever struggles we experience here on earth, we go through them in the strength of the one who has gone before us.

> [Jesus] endured the cross, scorning its shame, and sat down at the right hand of the throne of God. Consider him who endured such opposition from sinful men, so that you will not grow weary and lose heart.

This has to be a relevant and timely message for the countless millions of ordinary men and women today who feel oppressed and beaten down by life.

Jesus the Judge

It is sobering to remember that when he returns at the end of time, Jesus will come as our Lord and our Judge. On that day we will each have to bow the knee to him and account for how we have lived our lives. It would be very convenient if we knew the date of his return! We could make sure that we had prepared ourselves to meet him. But, though his return is definite, the day and the hour remain God's secret.

Those of us who have only ever thought of Jesus as our Friend and Comforter would do well to remember that he is also our Judge, lest we fall into the trap of overfamiliarity and fail to develop the respect he is due as the one to whom we are ultimately accountable. Jesus himself stressed the importance of this accountability, making it clear that it is an essential part of our relationship with him:

> 'Moreover, the Father judges no-one, but has entrusted all judgment to the Son, that all may honour the Son just as they

honour the Father. He who does not honour the Son does not
honour the Father, who sent him.'

Many of us compartmentalise our lives to such an extent that
judgement is seen as something in the future – distant, unreal,
in another time and place. But Christ's judgement is not just
destined for the end of history: it is ongoing, constant, *now*.
If our lives are not at one with his life, we will feel the sharp
sword of his judgement in our lives, our spirituality and our
ministry, *now*:

'I am the vine; you are the branches. If a man remains in me and
I in him, he will bear much fruit; apart from me you can do
nothing. If anyone does not remain in me, he is like a branch
that is thrown away and withers; such branches are picked up,
thrown into the fire and burned.'

Jesus is our Judge today and tomorrow, now and in eternity.
This has to be a part of our message to a fun-loving, hedonistic society where 'live now, pay later' is the rule. We
should not play it down. When we tell the story of Jesus, we
are inviting people to make room in their lives for confession,
repentance and a chance to make amends. Unpopular though
such a message may sound, it is an integral part of who Jesus
is and what we believe about him.

The evangelist's message

I used to believe in God as some vague cloud of power – mys-
terious, unknowable, distant. But when I discovered who
Jesus was, I discovered the true God who is 'I am'. One of the
great joys of becoming a Christian is that we come to know
Jesus personally and are drawn into the presence of God
through him. There are some days when the friendship of
Jesus is very real to me, days when he shares my burdens and
carries my load. And there are other days when I don't feel
him near at all. But even then I claim his promise that he will
never leave me nor forsake me:

> 'My sheep listen to my voice; I know them, and they follow me.
> I give them eternal life, and they shall never perish; no-one can
> snatch them out of my hand.'

As we seek to share the gospel with others, we must encourage them to listen out for his voice among all the clamouring voices of the world we live in. There is much that will alarm us in this fast-changing and stressful society, but his voice can still breathe its ancient peace into any situation. This is the voice they must know and follow, which will reassure them when things seem to be falling apart, and which will lead them on to eternal joy at the end of this transient life. This is the voice whose Word rings true behind our words. When I'm briefing mission teams, I still repeat the advice of the old-time evangelist Herbert Silverwood. 'Tell them about Jesus,' I say, 'because my experience has shown that even in a complex multi-cultural society, this is what they want to hear.'

Jesus strides across the centuries to us today to address our confusion, loss of direction and lack of meaning. His call to us, as to every generation, is simply, 'I am the way'. This isn't primarily an invitation to follow his teaching or to adopt a set of theological precepts. He is inviting us to share a relationship with him. He welcomes us as friends. This single relationship will have the most profound effect on our lives. Jesus will transform our priorities and change our perspectives. More than that, as we allow him to take over our lives he will actually redeem us, releasing us from slavery to our failure, our sinfulness and our selfishness. He will set us free. He will take our scars – the wounds that go deep into our past, the hurts, the disappointments, the regrets, the dark shadows that haunt us down the years – and heal them.

This is not a once-for-all experience. As we welcome Jesus into the different areas of our personality, we will see his ongoing work of redemption. In knowing him, loving him and communing with him, we discover that he meets those needs nothing else can reach; for he is the one who gave us life and to whom, one day, we must give account as to how we have lived it.

Jesus is at the centre of all we believe. He is what makes Christianity distinctive and is the reason behind our evangelism. Over the last fifteen years I have led 'Share Jesus' missions in hundreds of churches. As I go out on mission, the project's title always reminds me of the purpose for my going. I must *share Jesus*, nothing more and nothing less. In sharing him, I share the heart of the gospel message. This has rarely been a matter of going through a theological formula. Rather, it has usually been an opportunity to introduce them to my best friend. Introducing them to the church, the denomination or even the fellowship of local Christians is always secondary.

For far too long the word 'evangelism' has been a dirty word in the life of the church. We have talked 'mission', we have talked 'service' and we have talked 'political action', but many church leaders have avoided the evangelistic task Jesus commissioned us all to undertake. Statisticians tell us that most churches spend less time, money and energy on it than almost anything else they do. Post-modernism, with its emphasis on connecting with our roots and on 'being real' about what we believe poses many new challenges. Perhaps, above all, it gives us a wonderful opportunity to put evangelism back at the top of the agenda.

Bible references: Luke 1:35; Colossians 1:15–16; Luke 4:18–19; Matthew 20:25–28; John 13:1–17; Philippians 2:6–8; Matthew 13:53–58; Luke 4:14–30; 7:36–50; Matthew 23:37; Luke 19:1–10; John 4:1–26; Luke 17:11–19; John 3:16–17; Hebrews 12:2–3; John 5:22–23; 15:5–6; 10:27–28.

Chapter 2

SPIRIT-FILLED EVANGELISM

I recently visited Pensacola in Florida, where there has been a powerful move of the Holy Spirit over the last couple of years. More than 144,000 people have given their lives to Christ, and thousands more have experienced the renewal of the Holy Spirit in powerful ways. The focus of the revival has been the Assemblies of God church in one of the inner-city areas of Pensacola, called Brownsville; but the Methodist Church out in the suburbs at Pine Forest has also been deeply touched by this move of the Spirit.

The young people from the youth group were the first to attend the Brownsville revival meetings, but soon they dragged their parents along. Finally, Perry Dalton, the United Methodist pastor, went downtown to see what all the fuss was about! His own ministry was changed and renewed, and he began to call the local Methodist congregation to fasting and prayer. The Methodist folk were touched by the Holy Spirit, and it led to a painful and powerful time of confession, repentance and forgiveness. Families were brought together, marriages healed, parents and children reunited, and many deep pastoral situations brought out into the open for ministry through prayer and counselling. It wasn't all good news, however. About one-third of the congregation resigned their membership in protest at the change of emphasis and direction of their church. Nonetheless, as they left, many others, particularly those on the fringes of church life, came to take their place.

This was my second visit to Pine Forest, and on both

occasions my own life has been deeply challenged and my ministry renewed. When I preached there a year ago, I was fascinated to discover that they still had quite a traditional form of worship. There was a choir, robed altar boys and a fairly liturgical format. When I announced the first hymn and people stood up to sing, the presence of the Holy Spirit was almost tangible. By the second verse, four people were kneeling at the altar rail in floods of tears, wanting to confess their sins and get right with God. By the time I started to preach, the altar rail was full and the prayer team was at work among them. I turned to the pastor and asked if I should go on. He urged me to do so and, as I continued, yet more of the congregation came forward in repentance.

While there are many aspects of such a revival that I personally struggle with, and certain phenomena which bother me, I am left with one overwhelming emotion. If the Holy Spirit can renew a fairly traditional United Methodist Church in suburban Florida, he can do it anywhere!

Perhaps we have sanitised the Holy Spirit and made him too safe. Perhaps we prefer that he remain under our control rather than have free rein among us. Perhaps the form of Christianity found in many of our churches needs his refreshing power to shake us up and remind us whose church it really is! There was certainly nothing safe about the first Pentecost. Luke describes the arrival of the Spirit as like the 'blowing of a violent wind' which rushed through the house in which the disciples were meeting:

> They saw what seemed to be tongues of fire that separated and came to rest on each of them. All of them were filled with the Holy Spirit and began to speak in other tongues as the Spirit enabled them.

Scary stuff! Imagine the reaction of your local congregation if this happened on Sunday. Wow! Imagine it happening at your Parish Council, Elders Meeting or Leaders Committee?

Having experienced Pine Forest United Methodist Church

for myself, these things don't seem as impossible as they once were. But why would God do this? Why would he send the Holy Spirit to zap us in these new ways? Well, I don't believe he'd do it to give us a warm glow inside. I don't think he'd do it just to give us a pentecostal 'experience'. And I don't think he'd do it to get us dancing in the aisles. No. The Bible makes it clear that when God sends the Holy Spirit, he sends him to empower his people for mission.

- Jesus told his disciples that as the Father had sent him so he was sending them; then he breathed on them, telling them to receive the Holy Spirit. He was giving them power to fulfil his great commission, to 'go and make disciples of all nations'.

- On the day of Pentecost, when the disciples received the Holy Spirit, it wasn't followed by a seven-day revival convention. No. Immediately they began to communicate in the languages of the people gathered in Jerusalem, and to speak the gospel in ways that could be understood. He was giving them power to communicate.

- When the early church was looking for a group of people to engage in a work of practical ministry to care for those in need among them, what did they look for? Seven men 'known to be full of the Spirit and wisdom'. He gave them power to act.

What has all this to do with evangelism in the church today? Well, many local churches are struggling to fulfil the mission God has given us. Columnist Mary Kenny, writing in the *Guardian*, compared the death of traditional Christian denominations with the rise of Islam: 'What does British Islam offer in their place? Perhaps not much on the music front so far, but characteristics which seem to be draining out of some aspects of Christianity. Commitment. Conviction. Energy. Values. Belief. Certainty.' If we want to be really effective in evangelism, we need to wait on God for the renewing power of the Holy Spirit. We need to recognise that we cannot do this work in our own strength, and to admit that many of our strategies, plans and concepts aren't really working because they lack God's anointing upon them.

The Holy Spirit in the process of evangelism

Some time ago I visited Niagara Falls on the border between the United States and Canada. At the time it was possible to take a trip into the caves behind the Falls and to experience the thundering power of the water close up. I got togged up in a waterproof suit and edged my way along with the guide into the network of cavernous passages behind this massive waterfall. Eventually we arrived in a small chamber opening directly on to the centre of the Falls.

The roar was deafening and a fine sheet of spray filled the space where we were. Rainbows danced in the sunlight on every side. It was spectacular to look through the roaring torrent of water just a few metres away. The guide shouted above the noise, telling us that the chamber in which we were standing would one day house a hydro-electric power station. The waterfall would generate enough power to light up many of the northern states of the USA.

As I stood watching the waterfall from the inside, its power almost tangible around me, I began to think of the power of the Holy Spirit, which shaped the universe and brought creation out of chaos. Niagara Falls, by comparison, paled into insignificance! I began to look at the Holy Spirit in a different way. If he has the power to hold the cosmos together and to keep the planets swirling in their rightful orbit, what an enormous waste it is not to use that power to equip us for the task of evangelism!

Too much evangelism is done in the power of human personality and creativity, and not enough is done in the power of God. Too much evangelism ends up weak and ineffectual because it has failed to draw on the resources of the Holy Spirit. Yet it is his ministry we are engaging in; it is his task to convict men and women of sin and thus begin the process of conversion. The part we play simply involves enabling people to discover his renewing and transforming power in their lives.

In Romans chapter 8, Paul makes it clear that the Holy Spirit is active in the ongoing development of our relationship with God. A quick review of Romans chapter 8 shows that through him...

- We are set free from the law of sin and death. Without the help of the Holy Spirit we are powerless to do anything outside of our sinful nature *(vs 1–4)*.

- Our minds begin to tune in to what God wants. Through the activity of the Holy Spirit we are able to overcome the power of sin with all its deadly effects *(v 5)*.

- We discover the daily life which God wants us to enjoy. Only by the Spirit of God can we have victory over temptation and evil in our lives. In fact, without the Holy Spirit we cannot even belong to Christ *(vs 6–9)*.

- We receive the guarantee of eternal life, and know that the day will come when we will rise to live with Christ forever. But eternal life is not just for the future: it is an experience that begins when we follow Christ *(vs 10–11)*.

- We know how to live and what to do. The Spirit bears witness to the fact that we are God's children and gives us the confidence to approach him as '*Abba*, Father' *(vs 12–17)*.

How can we possibly engage in evangelism without recognising that it is the Holy Spirit's work? Evangelism is no more than us coming into partnership with him as he continues to do what he is already doing in people's lives. If we try to do evangelism without him, we will find it so much harder. We need the Spirit's power if we are to communicate with those who are blinded by the 'god of this age'. Even more, we need his discernment and authority if we are to break down spiritual strongholds and set people free:

> For though we live in the world, we do not wage war as the
> world does. The weapons we fight with are not the weapons of
> the world. On the contrary, they have divine power to demolish
> strongholds.

It has always fascinated me that, during the industrial revolution, the entrepreneurs of eighteenth-century Britain were able to discover different sources of power and use them for many purposes. I came across one small area near Manchester in which there had sprung up a snuff mill, a flour mill, a cotton mill and several other industrial factories. They were all driven by the same small river. It is God's power, the Holy Spirit, which should drive and energise all activity in Christ's Name. If we try to do evangelism in our own strength, we are wasting the power God has made available to us.

How ludicrous that we should even think of engaging in evangelism without working with the creative power of God! How strange that we should try to evangelise without the Spirit whose work it really is! How ridiculous that we should try to evangelise without using the driving force he has given specifically for the task!

The Holy Spirit in the life of the church

Before his Ascension, Jesus instructed his disciples to wait in Jerusalem until they had received the promised power of God. This power was given so that they could fulfil his commission to go into all the world to make new followers.

One of the hallmarks of a group of believers who are empowered by the Holy Spirit is the quality of their life together. The early church in Jerusalem can give us a clear example of a such a group:

- The Christians in Jerusalem were known for their unity,
  their friendship, their willingness to share everything
  with one another and their concern for others.

- They were known for their ability to bring people to Christ, and for their effectiveness in looking after those new converts and drawing them into the life of the church.

- The Jerusalem Christians had a strong sense of unity and a powerful prayer life.

- They did not tolerate sinfulness.

- They were committed to the growth and development of new work.

- Many believe that the church in Jerusalem grew by thousands of people in the early months of its existence. This growth was surely a witness to its health as a fellowship.

The Jerusalem Christians were truly effective in evangelism because theirs was a church empowered by the Spirit. Their life together paints a vivid picture of what a truly evangelistic group of Christians should look like.

The Holy Spirit in power evangelism

Jesus ushered in the kingdom of God by demonstrating his authority over the supernatural world, disease and death. He cast out demons, healed those who were sick, made the blind see, the lame walk and the deaf hear. He commanded nature's obedience by stilling the storm and walking on water. He raised people from the dead to new life. Likewise, the apostles were known not only for their preaching and good works, but also for their ability to perform miracles and thus demonstrate that the power of God really works. In Philip's ministry, we see this clearly illustrated:

> When the crowds heard Philip and saw the miraculous signs he did, they all paid close attention to what he said.

Power evangelism relies on direct intervention by God in the lives of ordinary people. It recognises God's sovereign ability to break into our world with signs and wonders and miracles. John Wimber once commented, 'In pragmatic evangelism we say something and God acts, but in power evangelism God says something and we act.' In this kind of outreach, demonstration and proclamation go hand in hand.

In my travels around the world I have come across many situations in which power evangelism has been mightily used by God – incredible healings, the miraculous arrival of rain, the dramatic conversion of violent criminals. I have not seen much power evangelism at work in my own ministry, and have sometimes wondered what kind of effect miraculous events would have in such a cynical secularised culture as the one in which we live in the UK. I was deeply challenged by the testimony of a newly retired secondary school headmaster in a tough area of London. He confessed to me that he only really discovered that prayer works towards the end of his teaching career. He had become bored and fed up with a form of Christianity which seemed to lack credibility and power, so he started to 'put God to the test'. He told of incident after incident during the stressful years of leading a large school community, in which he dared to pray for miracles and told his staff and students that he was doing so. It was little wonder, therefore, that when his prayers began to be answered in the lives of individuals and of the whole community, people began to listen to him. They became hungry to know more about 'faith that works'.

The Holy Spirit in renewal and revival

Some Christians argue that we don't need evangelism, we need revival. They look to God to 'do the job for us' and 'bring the people back to church'. Sadly, I fear that many of them don't really understand the nature of revival. Historically, revival is about what happens in the church before anything can happen in the world!

A W Tozer pointed out that many churches do need revival. The telltale signs of this need were, in his opinion, 'Rut, rote and rot'. There are many such church groups around today. They are bound up and lacking direction, religious but without any sense of understanding or reality in their faith. They expect nothing to happen and have no vision for reaching the lost.

> We can define revival as a period of unusual blessing and activity in the church. A revival is something that happens first in the church and among Christian people. When the life of a church begins to wane, to droop and has almost become moribund it needs revival! Revival means awakening, stimulating the life, bringing it to the surface again. It happens primarily in the church of God. *(Dr Martyn Lloyd-Jones)*

There are countless examples down the centuries of the reviving power of the Holy Spirit touching the lives of ordinary Christians and empowering them to evangelise the world.

In 1722, a small group of Christians in Germany met on the estate of Count Nikolaus von Zinzendorf. There they encountered the Holy Spirit in a powerful way. Their hearts were set aflame with a new love for Jesus Christ and for one another. They began to meet in prayer more regularly and, on 25 August 1727, they established a 'round-the-clock' prayer meeting which ran, uninterrupted, for a hundred years. At every moment of the day and night there were people praying. Out of this was born a mission to evangelise many unreached peoples. Tens of thousands of people became Christians through the ministry of these evangelists.

On 1 January 1739, John Wesley and about sixty of his fellowship were praying deep into the night. He wrote in his diary:

> About three in the morning, as we were continuing constant in prayer, the power of God came mightily upon us insomuch that many cried out for exceeding joy and many fell to the ground. As soon as we were recovered a little from that awe and amazement at the presence of His majesty we broke out with one voice – 'We praise Thee, O God, we acknowledge Thee to be the Lord.'

As a result of this empowering, and the 'strangely warmed heart' of John Wesley, revival flooded across the United Kingdom.

In 1857, Jeremiah Lanphier, a city missioner in New York, gave out handbills inviting fellows Christians to join him in prayer for the nation. On 23 September that year, just six people took up his invitation. A week later twenty came; the following week forty. The meetings grew so popular that he had to hold them daily. Within five months there were three prayer meetings happening simultaneously in large theatres in the city. Soon similar gatherings for prayer were happening in Boston, Chicago, Washington, Buffalo and Newark. Thousands gathered each day to pray for the spiritual renewal of the United States. In Portland, Oregon, the meetings grew so popular that 240 major stores closed each day between 11 o'clock in the morning and 2 o'clock in the afternoon to enable their employees to pray. Natural and spontaneous evangelism flowed from the tens of thousands of Christians caught up in this renewal of faith. Historians estimate that there were over one million new converts to Christ in 1858–59!

Meanwhile, back in the United Kingdom, Charles Haddon Spurgeon was not only teaching about prayer, he was modelling the truth that prayer is integral to evangelism. Wherever he went, he called the church to prayer, teaching that it was the springboard for all true mission and ministry. Whenever guests visited him at his church, the Metropolitan Tabernacle, he would show them the prayer-room where church members continued a 24-hour unceasing vigil of prayer. Out of this renewed sense of commitment to prayer in the churches arose a great wave of evangelistic activity. Church historians estimate that there were around one million new converts to Christianity in Britain during 1860 alone. Out of this came new leaders such as Lord Shaftesbury, George Muller and William Booth.

Following five years of dedicated prayer by a small group of missionaries in the Philippines, a retired pastor, Paul

Holsinger, called the people of his church to repentance and reconciliation. The congregation was suddenly and powerfully renewed with the Holy Spirit and, as a result, hundreds of local townspeople were converted to Christianity. The revival swept from town to town. Even now, decades later, there is incredible church growth all across that region.

In Korea, possibly the best known example of contemporary revival, experts suggest that 110,000 of the population were converted in 1982, and 120,000 in 1983. Pastor Yonggi Cho, leader of one of the fastest growing 'super churches' in the region, said, 'We have seen the importance of developing and keeping a prayer life. If we stop praying the revival will wane. If we continue praying, I believe that all Korea can be saved!'

In the UK, sporadic and limited bursts of revival have continued up to the present day. Tom Wilson, a leading gypsy revivalist, told a capacity crowd at the Royal Albert Hall of revival among the gypsy population. A thousand gypsies came to Christ in a period of a few weeks in Scotland, and in less than a decade at least ten thousand have come to Christ across the country.

In England, local volunteers from the Prison Fellowship had long desired to do work in tough Lewes prison. Unable to find opportunities, they decided to walk round the outside of the jail, praying for the spiritual walls to come down. They prayed regularly and consistently for ten years. Eventually David Lowe was appointed as prison chaplain and, alongside the Prison Fellowship, they began evangelistic work in the prison. Over a two-year period, over 500 inmates, their relatives and prison officers have made professions of faith in Christ. The *Daily Telegraph* commented: 'In the last 12 months fights between inmates have dropped dramatically. Half the prisoners "touched by the Spirit" have written to apologise to their victims.' The newspaper went on to say that similar experiences of revival are reported in ten other British prisons.

Overseas we hear of waves of renewal sweeping across the

church, affecting tens of thousands of people in places like Toronto and Pensacola. God seems to be breaking down the structures of formalised institutional religion and inviting his people to meet him in new and uncluttered ways through miraculous demonstrations of his power. I believe there will be many more waves of spiritual renewal in the new millennium, each one calling us to move beyond the familiar trappings of our comfortable Christianity to meet God face to face. It is this kind of spiritual renewal that will enable ordinary people to discover the spiritual reality they crave, and empower them to share the message in new ways that are both relevant and creative.

A number of common factors can be found in these great periods of growth in Christianity. Each seems to have been preceded by the raising up of groups to pray and intercede. Each seems to have brought forward rebellious young leaders with a heart for evangelism, people like George Whitefield (aged 22), Howell Harris in Wales (aged 25) and John Wesley (aged 36). Each manifests a renewed search for holiness, a mass movement in prayer, the re-emergence of authoritative biblical preaching, and the introduction of new and radical methods of outreach and evangelism. There is, however, a danger.

The eighteenth-century established church was united in its suspicion of 'enthusiasm', a term that meant much the same as 'fanatic' today, which they applied to anyone whose practice of Christianity manifested any fervour. Such religion was considered to be a threat to the peace of the realm. They preferred religion to be quietly dispassionate. This view was rejected by John Wesley, who opposed the dependence on reason his Anglican contemporaries so advocated. However, he also recognised the danger of relying too much on feelings. Wesley chose instead a middle way, one that expressed an awesome respect for the Bible, but interpreted in the light of reason, church tradition and personal experience. His evangelistic fervour and his advocacy of 'the strangely warmed heart' challenged the cold deism of the established church, but he fiercely protected his followers from the fanaticism England had seen in the previous century.

Similarly, church leaders of the new millennium must guard the flock lest feelings become more important than the Bible. While the society of the new millennium may hunger for miraculous demonstrations of God's power, we must ensure that these are based on the unchanging and eternal facts of the gospel of Jesus Christ.

Without the power of the Holy Spirit in evangelism, the work is impossible. Without prayer, evangelism is a waste of time. This is God's work and it would be presumptuous and futile to imagine we can do it without him.

Bible references: Acts 2:3–4; John 20:21–22; Matthew 28:19–20; Acts 6:3; John 16:8–14; 2 Corinthians 4:4; 10:3–4; Acts 1:4–5; 2:42–47; 4:32–37; 5:1–11; 6:1–7; 8:6.

Book references: John Wimber and Kevin Springer, *Power Healing*, Hodder and Stoughton, 1986.

Chapter 3

GOD-GUIDED EVANGELISM

In the last two chapters we have seen that our message should be Jesus-focused and our methods Spirit-anointed. The third foundational principle about evangelism is that our motivation should be God-centred. Our heavenly Father sees the big picture. He knows history from before the start of time to after its close. He understands us better than we understand ourselves. He is working his purposes out in ways far beyond our comprehension. In doing evangelism, therefore, we become partners in an activity God undertakes through us.

Any time

It was a dark, wintry afternoon and the snow was cascading down. I was out on my pastoral visits in the mining village where I was a local minister. I had spent three hours visiting the sick and the elderly, and it was nearly time to go home. It was my last call of the afternoon. I swallowed the strong brew of tea, and placed the fragile cup and saucer on the table. I bade the frail old lady farewell and trudged through the snow to my car.

The roads were treacherous and the wheels on my car slithered as I drove through the snow. It was clear we were in for a bad night. At the end of the road I got a strong feeling that I should go and visit an elderly man. However, I felt very tired and I had another meeting later in the evening. I was looking forward to a break. I stopped the car, pulled the handbrake on, leant back and sighed. I really didn't want to bother. I sat and analysed the feeling. I wondered if I was going mad. Maybe I was overtired or trapped by some guilt-complex. Or maybe God was trying to tell me something.

I was convinced this old man didn't really need a visit. He was quite well and surely wouldn't expect me to call on such a snowy afternoon. Several moments passed as I tried to make a decision. At last I gave in. Instead of turning left towards home, I turned right toward this man's house. By now the snow was falling in great white clumps, and the car laboured as I drove up the steep hill toward the council estate where he lived. I went in through the gate and knocked on the back door, as was the custom in our mining village. The old man greeted me warmly and put the kettle on. Soon I was consuming yet another cup of hot strong tea. We talked about many things, and I ended by sharing my faith about Jesus. I prayed for him before I left. I went home wondering why I'd been to see him. It made no sense at all and, as I drove back through the snow, I felt a little resentful that my time-off before the evening meeting had been cut so short.

Late that night, however, the old man died unexpectedly of a heart attack. I was one of the last people to speak to him. If I hadn't trusted my gut feeling and gone to visit him, I think I'd have lived the rest of my life with a tinge of regret.

I am sure God guides us. If we are really listening to him and are sensitive to his prompting, he will help us to be in the right place at the right time, saying the right thing. Over the years I have come to realise that God-centred evangelism may mean a call to action at the most inconvenient moments. God has sometimes overturned my list of priorities, interrupted my social life or made me late for important engagements. He has sometimes had to overrule my diary or my schedule so that he can lead me into situations that are ripe for evangelism. His will doesn't always fit neatly around my plans!

If we really want to be effective in evangelism, we must be willing to say 'anytime' to the Lord, and that means taking down the barriers around our schedule and letting him be Lord of *all* our time. Sadly, there are many Christians who fence off areas of their lives from the sovereign will of God, who have never made the connection between evangelism and their life. But Jesus made it clear that commitment to him was not easy and that following him may involve us in costly decisions:

'If anyone would come after me, he must deny himself and take up his cross daily and follow me. For whoever wants to save his life will lose it, but whoever loses his life for me will save it.'

There is a great freedom in giving over all of our time to God. Suddenly we are available to be used in situations we might previously have considered unlikely fields for evangelism, and miss out on some of the most rewarding opportunities God has in store.

The story of Philip and the Ethiopian official convinces me of the importance of submitting my plans and activities to God's guiding. Philip was in the middle of his big mission in a city in Samaria. The days had been packed with action, with large crowds at the meetings, miraculous signs, amazing healings and hundreds coming to Christ. The whole community had been influenced by the mission and 'there was great joy in that city'. Here was fertile ground for serving the Lord and furthering the gospel. Philip might well have wondered if it could be bettered. Then 'an angel of the Lord said to Philip, "Go south to the road – the desert road – that goes down from Jerusalem to Gaza." '

It must have seemed a bit of a come-down, standing by that desert road in the middle of nowhere. Philip may have wondered what he could possibly achieve. It must have seemed a far better use of his time to have stayed in Samaria. But just then, over the horizon, came a chariot bearing an Ethiopian treasury official – one man struggling to understand the meaning of scripture. At once Philip saw the purpose of his journey, but still it must have seemed rather mundane after the signs and wonders of his city mission. Nevertheless, he went ahead and did what he felt God was asking him to do: he got alongside the man, 'began with that very passage of Scripture and told him the good news about Jesus'. The outcome was immediate and positive: the Ethiopian accepted the gospel and was baptised. But that was all Philip was to see: 'the Spirit of the Lord suddenly took Philip away, and the eunuch did not see him again, but went on his way rejoicing'.

God-centred evangelism puts God on the throne and ourselves at his service. When we engage in God-centred evangelism, we are not doing something special: we are only fulfilling what he expects of us. Of course, this style of Christian living is costly, yet it opens us up to being in the centre of the Lord's will. When we allow each day to be fully his, we ourselves become fully his. At last we can honestly say to the Lord that we are wholly available.

There are some teachers you never forget. When I was a teenager, one of my college lecturers was a tall, bearded man with an unapproachable manner. He was always reciting his favourite motto: 'You have all of my sympathy, but none of my time'. He lived by what he said: it was hard to talk to him because he was always rushing off somewhere. I didn't want his sympathy, but I often needed a few moments of his time. But he was always too busy.

I'm sure that many of us have so filled our lives with 'important' activities that we are not available to respond to God's call. Day after day we rush from one place to the next, offering everyone we meet 'all of our sympathy but none of our time'. Some of us are moving through life at such a speed that we meet people but don't get to know them. We hear people but don't listen to them. We look at people but don't see their need. We miss opportunities for evangelism with those around us. We say to the Lord, 'Anytime, but not just now!' The Lord sends people into our lives for many reasons but, sadly, we sometimes regard them as 'interruptions' to our busy schedule. In doing so, we are missing out on wonderful opportunities for witness. We have not discovered the joy and excitement of engaging in God-centred evangelism.

Anywhere

One of my college mates used to say, 'Here comes Rob, always in the wrong place at the wrong time.' He only meant it as a joke but there was a sharp edge to what he said as well! If we are to engage in God-centred evangelism, we must allow him to put us where we can be properly useful to him. A crucial part of our Christian commitment is to say, 'Anywhere you send me, Lord, I will go.' For some people, that kind of commitment will mean a move to the other side of the world; for others, it will mean staying just where they are.

This is vividly illustrated by the story of Jonah. He certainly had to learn this lesson the hard way. When God asked him to go and preach to the people of Nineveh, he didn't want to go. Nineveh was a pagan city and he knew he would not be welcome there. So Jonah decided on a compromise. He agreed to uproot and travel overseas, but *he* would choose the location. So he set sail for Tarshish. However, he never stopped to think through the consequences: that by stepping out of the Lord's will, he would end up in the wrong place at the wrong time and be totally ineffective.

We all know what happened next. The boat hit stormy weather, and Jonah was thrown into the sea and consumed by a great fish. There, in the belly of the fish, he asked God for forgiveness and offered himself totally. God forgave him, and Jonah went to prophecy in the place God had ordained for his mission. It certainly wasn't an easy assignment – perhaps it wasn't what he would have planned for himself – but it was God's place. And, because he was in the right place at the right time, God blessed his ministry there:

> The Ninevites believed God. They declared a fast, and all of them, from the greatest to the least, put on sackcloth...
>
> When God saw what they did and how they turned from their evil ways, he had compassion and did not bring upon them the destruction he had threatened.

We cannot plan our own lives in the Lord's service. We cannot choose the opportunities *we* think are best or the places *we* think are 'right'. We must actively seek God's will and submit ourselves to it if we want to be effective in his service.

To be in the right place at the right time may involve us in pain or persecution. God's will for our lives does not always mean an easy time; in fact it may lead us into very difficult situations. This was highlighted for me when I visited a small town in Eastern Europe during the days of the cold war, when Communism still reigned. It was good to meet the Christians there and to work with the local minister for several weeks. It was good to be away from the tourist track and to sample the everyday life of the townspeople. My friend, the minister, spoke fluent English, so he was able to act as interpreter. Through him I talked for hours with the local Christians. One group of teenagers told me about the subtle forms of persecution they encountered. Some found it impossible to get a grant for college because they were Christians; others talked of closed career prospects and trouble with the authorities. I was impressed by their strong faith and their willingness to stay faithful to Jesus Christ, whatever the cost. I wished that some of my youth group could hear them talk.

A little later I met a very elderly minister. 'The trouble is,' he said, 'you have many young believers in the West, but I don't think their faith is very strong. Would they still follow Jesus if they had to pay the cost that our young people pay?' I looked at his drawn face and asked him if he'd ever thought of leaving that country and coming to serve Christ in the West. He seemed hurt by my suggestion and paused to think through his reply. Then he bent forward and, with piercing eyes, asked, 'What would happen to the sheep if all the shepherds ran away?'

For my friend in the East, being in the right place meant staying just where he was. It would have been easy to run away to an easier climate and a ministry under less pressure. It can sometimes be harder to stay put for God. If we want to engage in God-centred evangelism, we must be willing to go anywhere to serve him, be it down the street or across the world. If we are open to his call, we can't put limits on where he might send us. In every season of our lives and every day of our busy schedule, our prayer must be, 'Lord, let me be in the right place at the right time.'

Anyone

I fumbled for the keys to the minibus. It was dark, and the rain was pouring down. The gang of teenage lads was getting restless. I opened the rear door and let them in. They had been quite well-behaved during the youth meeting, but now they were in high spirits. It was time to head for home. We drove away from the Hackney church into the stream of London traffic.

The journey back to Deptford wasn't an easy one. My passengers seemed determined to make it memorable! They rocked the minibus from side to side, made rude faces out of the rear window and sang bawdy songs at the top of their voices. I soon reached the limits of my patience, so I pulled onto the verge and gave them a stern warning – they could either shut up or start walking! On we went through the Rotherhithe tunnel and along the dark south London streets. As we drew up outside the church in Deptford where I worked, I sighed with relief.

Just as I was letting my passengers out, the tubby care-taker of the church burst through the church doors. 'You lot are in big trouble – you've really done it now!' he told us. 'If you're not all back in Hackney in thirty minutes, you'll have to face the police.'

The young people let out a loud groan of disapproval. I turned the vehicle round and headed back towards Hackney. An air of gloom descended on the group, and they all fell silent.

Walter, the Hackney minister, greeted us at the door of the church. 'Look, lads,' he explained. 'There's a wallet gone missing and an old man is very upset because it contained his money and his pension book. Okay, a joke's a joke. Let's have it back and the matter need go no further.'

There was an uneasy silence. The lads looked at each other as they tried to work out whether to speak or keep silent. The silence continued for several minutes, then one of them said, 'It's in the gent's toilet – third cistern along. We didn't mean anything by it.'

Walter went off to look, and returned a few minutes later with the dripping wallet held high. The lads apologised, if rather half-heartedly, and Walter beamed at us.

As the group boarded the minibus again, I went back and apologised. I felt responsible and I was really fed up. Perhaps I should close the youth club down – it all seemed such a pointless waste of time.

Walter took one look at me and roared with laughter. 'Why on earth are you looking like that? This is nothing! You should see some of the scrapes I've landed myself in. I've spent most of my ministry chasing badly behaved kids around church premises. But that's what it's all about. The minute we stop caring for kids like these, we might as well give up!'

I knew he was right and, over the years, I've remembered his advice when I've been in worse situations. It isn't easy to care for young people who vandalise church premises, who prefer clubbing to conversation, who disappear whenever you need their help. It really saddens me when I hear of youth leaders or churches who have 'given up on the young people'. They have turned their backs on a great opportunity for evangelism and witness. Only recently I heard that a youth club was closed down because a mirror had been broken. The church council ruled that these youngsters were no longer welcome on church premises because they 'broke too much, didn't pay enough, and were too badly behaved'. They had closed the door on an important opportunity for God-centred evangelism.

If we are realistic, we all know people with whom we find it hard to get on. They may not have the same interests as us or they may just see things very differently. Sometimes when we open the front door to someone like that, it's hard to seem pleased to see them. The temptation is to make some excuse and get rid of them as quickly as we can.

It can be costly to say, 'Anyone you send, Lord, I will love and be a witness to', for he may just ask us to serve those who have hurt us deeply and even scarred our lives. But Jesus taught that we should love our enemies and pray for those who persecute us:

> 'If you love those who love you, what reward will you get? Are not even the tax collectors doing that? And if you greet only your brothers, what are you doing more than others? Do not even pagans do that?'

Ananias was a man willing to reach out and forgive, no matter what the cost. He was a committed Christian living in Damascus and a good witness for the Lord. One day he heard that Saul of Tarsus, the enemy of the church, was on his way to town. This proud Jew was coming to break up the church and throw all the Christians into jail. A terrifying prospect!

Then Ananias felt the Lord calling him to go and witness to Saul. It must have seemed like he was asking rather a lot – after all, such a meeting could cost Ananias his life. It would probably have seemed wiser to go into hiding until Saul left town. But Ananias obeyed and went to the house where Saul was staying. His knees must have been knocking as he went in! Yet the first words Ananias spoke were 'Brother Saul'. He was willing to leave behind his anger and fear, and reach out to the person who threatened him most.

Saul was in dire need of Ananias' compassion. On his way to Damascus, he had had an extraordinary meeting with the Lord and been blinded during the encounter. He was wandering, confused, in that no-man's-land between conviction and conversion. Ananias was able to care for him and witness to him. As a result, Saul became a Christian. He was baptised and renamed Paul, and went on to become the greatest missionary the church has ever known – all because Ananias cared for his enemy!

God-centred evangelism is about being willing to witness to those we find difficult, those who have wronged us, even those against whom we hold prejudices. Over the years, I have attended courses on racism awareness and seen people who had refused to admit they were racist finally being made aware of their prejudice. Our prejudices are often only camouflaged by a veneer of politeness. Jesus had the knack of seeing right through that veneer. He mixed with the outcasts of his generation and seemed to care most for the people society rejected. Wherever our prejudices lie, we should be aware that the Lord has a habit of sending to us just the kind of person we would really rather not see!

> Though I am free and belong to no man, I make myself a slave to everyone, to win as many as possible ... I have become all things to all men so that by all possible means I might save some.

This statement was not an easy one for Paul to make. He was a Jew born of the tribe of Benjamin, trained by Gamaliel, a celebrated doctor of the Jewish law; and, what was more, he was a Pharisee, one of the Jewish elite. He had everything going for him in the Jewish society from which he came. It was unthinkable for someone from such a social background to mix with people of other races, let alone love them and serve them like a slave! Yet Paul was willing to count his privileged background as nothing for the sake of serving Christ. He had to ditch his feelings of superiority and start getting alongside people where they were.

Full obedience to Christ leads to real effectiveness in witness. God-centred evangelism is about being available anytime, anywhere and to anyone, taking the limits off our evangelism so that 'by all possible means we might save some'. There is a world of difference between the evangelist and the encyclopaedia salesman, between the Christian who shares the eternal love of God and the insurance rep selling life policies. We are participating in God's work and its results can only fully be measured in eternity. If we are to be effective in evangelism, we must submit ourselves whole-heartedly to the love and will of our heavenly Father. If we are not wholly available, we cannot usefully participate in fulfilling the purposes of our Sovereign God. We haven't said, 'Any time, anywhere, anyone.'

Bible references: Luke 9:23–24; Acts 8:4–8,26–39; Jonah 3:5–10; Matthew 5:46–47; Acts 9:1–19; 1 Corinthians 9:19,22.

Chapter 4

PERSON-TO-PERSON EVANGELISM

When I was a student at university, I was very hard up financially. In sheer desperation, I applied for a job with an American company which promised high rewards to anyone who was confident, approachable and friendly. When I arrived for my first day at the new job, I discovered that it actually entailed selling encyclopaedias!

After an intensive and emotional four-hour training course, we were divided into teams and allocated prosperous suburban housing estates within a thirty-mile radius of the regional office. As a 'trainee sales consultant', I followed a successful salesman from house to house and watched as he went through his well-rehearsed patter. It was fascinating. Within seconds of any door opening he had sized up the situation and tailored his pitch to match. Once he gained entry to a house, he generally found that he had a one-in-four chance of making the sale and charging in excess of one thousand pounds for a set of books.

I had three major misgivings about the technique, misgivings which became so disturbing that after three days I gave up the job. First, the salesman viewed each person as a target. They weren't people to him and he had no concern as to whether they needed what he was selling or, indeed, if they could really afford it. Second, he had a script which he recited. It was learnt by rote and, therefore, did not represent a true engagement with the people he was visiting. If at any point his 'client' tried to make him deviate from the script, he was quite unable to cope. Third, he had no time for people who didn't want to buy the product. At five points during his presentation he asked a question. A negative response to any of these meant that he was wasting his time and he would leave. As a committed Christian, I found this way of communicating with people unhealthy: it began to make me look at others in a way that was unscrupulous and lacking in compassion. It was a very hard way to earn a living.

A few months later I went on a training course in personal evangelism hosted by an Anglican church near my hall of residence. During the day we were taught a kind of patter very similar to that demonstrated by the encyclopaedia salesman. The same feelings of unease and disquiet began to return. Over the years since then I have come across a number of similar evangelistic strategies which have claimed great results. Based on similar concepts to those employed by sects such as the Jehovah's Witnesses and Mormons, and by the encyclopaedia salesmen, individual Christians are taught a 'patter'. During the course of door-to-door visits, they target potential converts and treat them like potential customers. This, to me, is not true evangelism, nor is it the kind of human relationship Jesus modelled.

I believe that 'evangelism by rote' can do more harm than good if we treat people in this way. It can bring dishonour to the people of God and be a disservice to the work of the gospel. The most effective form of evangelism is friendship evangelism, which involves sharing the gospel in real and powerful human relationships. Sadly, there are millions of Christians who do not have the know-how, the confidence or the experience to share their faith story in this way. There is a dormant army of evangelists waiting to be awoken for service in God's kingdom!

Some of us are naturally gifted in communicating with others, while others have to work very hard at it. Non-verbal communication is as important as the words we speak. Experts tell us that generally words make up 7%, tone of voice 38% and body language 55% of the content of our communication. So when people are listening to us, they are

45

taking in much more than the words we are saying. Our posture, volume level, dress, speed of speech, appearance and attitude are all important too. Do we sound angry or patronising, for example? It doesn't matter how good our message is, if we have an off-putting manner or aren't sharing honestly from the reality of who we are, we can't be effective in personal evangelism.

If we look at the way Jesus spoke to people, and the value and respect he accorded each individual, we will begin to see how important this is. One example is his encounter with the Samaritan woman at the well. Jesus knew how to break the ice – he asked her for a drink. He asked open questions like 'What do you want?' His conversation was full of interesting stories and illustrations. He showed her that he was interested in her as a person.

There are many different levels of human conversation. At the lowest level there is the 'How are you?' type of chat, which may happen when you meet a colleague in the corridor or another parent at the school gate, for example. This is usually shallow and we don't really expect an honest answer. Then there's the 'Have you heard about?' level in which we shelter behind facts about others and bits of gossip. We give nothing away about ourselves and learn little about anyone else. The third level is 'In my opinion...': we begin to risk sharing something of our ideas, opinions and decisions. The moment the other person disagrees, we will probably retract and retreat to safer ground. Real communication is about more than having opinions, and at the fourth level we begin to share our feelings and reveal something of our true selves. At the fifth and deepest level, however, we remove the mask and begin to trust others with the inner secrets of our lives as we open up to each other. It is this level, in my experience, which offers the best context for sharing the Christian message. Strangely enough, one can reach this level of conversation with another person surprisingly quickly or dreadfully slowly. It can sometimes take years of regular contact with someone before a sufficient level of trust grows up, but I have sometimes known it happen in minutes!

I don't know what it is about trains, but they are often the best environments for moving along the relationship scale very quickly. Perhaps it is the anonymity of the journey and the fact that you are unlikely ever to meet each other again. I was once travelling alone on a near-empty train when an elderly man came down the corridor and asked if he could sit next to me. I was somewhat noncommittal because I was fairly tired and had relished the idea of some personal space. Within minutes he was telling me that he had been a World War 2 bomber pilot, and that he was returning from the funeral of one of his lifelong friends who had been his co-pilot on many dangerous missions. We went quickly into a very deep level of sharing. Life, death, time, regret, forgiveness and God were all very much on the agenda. I had a God-given opportunity to share my faith, beginning where this man was and with his questions about life after death. Strangers on a train chatting about life's journey.

Statistics show that very few people become Christians by just turning up at church and accepting the faith: for most, it is a slow process. We are living in a highly secularised society, and we sometimes have to start off by just being 'shop windows' for the Lord long before others will want to know more. A friend of mine, who is now vicar of a large church in central London, became a Christian during his stay with a Christian family overseas. They never spoke directly to him about Jesus, but he gradually became aware that Jesus lived in that home. It was by looking at their lives and experiencing the quality of their relationships that he was drawn to faith in Jesus himself.

John Finney's well respected survey, *Finding Faith Today* (The Bible Society, 1992), revealed that for 39% of men and 40% of women a Christian friend was an important supportive factor in their coming to faith. For 15% of men the *main* factor in their becoming Christians was the influence of a friend, and for women it was even higher at 24%. Christian friends are important, according to Finney's research, because they give 'love, understanding, care and prayers'.

When Jesus met him, Zacchaeus was not a popular man. He was considered a traitor because, as a tax collector, he was regarded as a Roman collaborator. Yet Jesus was willing to go to Zacchaeus' home and become his friend. Sometimes as Christians we can appear proud, judgemental and 'stand-offish' to others. It is easy to categorise people in our dealings with them, to look on them as 'non-Christians' rather than 'not-yet-Christians'. However, our attitude should be one that wants to accompany them on the journey of faith rather than condemn them for not having any faith at all.

To many Christians, the big question about friendship evangelism is the most embarrassing: 'Have you got any non-Christian friends?' Some of the most frustrating experiences I have ever had as an evangelist stemmed from this problem. It would appear that there are churches around with congregations who have hardly any non-Christian friends. It is little wonder, then, that evangelism seems impossible! Where can they begin?

When someone becomes a Christian, they often want to leave their non-Christian friends behind and devote themselves to the life of their fellowship. That's so unfortunate, because their friendship network could be such a rich seam for personal evangelism. We must encourage new Christians to be witnesses for Jesus in the context of their ordinary life rather than leave it all behind for the sacred sanctuary of the fellowship!

We have to earn the right to talk about Jesus, and one of the ways we can do this is by caring. It is because we care that people will listen. I teach this aspect of mission to our year-long Seed Team members at the beginning of their annual orientation course. It is remarkable what stories they bring back with them to their first residential conference several months later. One team discovered that a neighbour had lost her dog. They responded by showing the woman a deep sense of compassion and care during what was for her a very real time of crisis. They helped to prepare 'lost dog' posters which were attached to lampposts all over the area, and they went out searching the neighbourhood with a photo of the dog. It was eventually found and the woman did more to advance evangelism on the estate than a thousand glossy handbills!

Another team began to hang around a local park, even buying skateboards to become part of the local 'teen scene'. They gained such skill in skateboarding, they earned some street-cred and influence. One evening I visited their home and was impressed to see a line of skateboards all the way up the garden path, while inside the skateboarders were having their weekly Bible study.

A third team noticed that local residents often had to queue for long periods before they could collect their pensions and benefits from the post office. They opened up the church hall and served free tea and coffee, building bridges with people and opening the way for the Christian message.

When we knock on someone's door demanding a hearing, we have often not taken the time to care or the trouble to understand. If personal evangelism is to be effective, it must be set in the context of real, caring human relationships. When we care for the old man who is shut-in, his neighbours will surely hear about it. When we care for the harassed young mum struggling to bring up a child alone, she will tell other mums at the school gate. When we care for the young people gathering in the park at night, their parents may well sigh with relief. Caring prepares the way for the gospel more effectively than the most dynamic mission programme. We must show that Christianity works *before* we try to persuade others of its credibility. And this caring is not just preparation for evangelism: rather, it flows out of a deep sense of compassion for others given to us by the Lord.

Personal evangelism without caring can appear hard and heartless. Mission without compassion lacks the integrity and authenticity of the gospel. The most effective personal evangelism is to be someone's friend – and not just a 'fair-weather' friend, but a committed, caring and compassionate friend; someone who can be relied upon, come what may. Our great privilege is to introduce them to our Friend, who will accept them no matter where they've been, what they've done, how they've lived or who they are; and who will begin a new life within them.

Every committed Christian should have a concern for at least three or four non-Christian friends. When our mission teams go out, I ask them to produce a 'personal constituency' – a sheet of paper listing the non-Christian people for whom they are praying and with whom they are sharing the gospel. It is fascinating to hear how names added to the list sometimes become friends, and out of those friendships come new disciples. I would encourage every Christian to maintain such a list. It provides a focus for personal evangelism and reminds us that we are all, in a sense, on mission all of the time.

Some years ago a friend of mine was on a train travelling from Leeds to Birmingham. As he walked down the corridor, he prayed about where he should sit, and finally took a seat opposite a rather bored-looking woman. He began to talk to her about late-running trains, the weather and life in general. By the time the train reached Birmingham he had shared his testimony and taken out his Bible to share some verses about Jesus. When the train arrived in Birmingham, however, he had to get off to attend a meeting. Frustrated that the conversation wasn't over, my friend gave the woman his Bible and wrote his address in the cover in case she might like to write and ask him more.

Completely unbeknown to him, a Christian got on at Birmingham and looked for somewhere to sit. As she walked down the carriage she saw a lady reading a Bible, so she sat down opposite her. She began to ask her fellow passenger about her faith and soon discovered this woman's hunger to know more. By the time the train had arrived in Plymouth, this passenger had found Jesus Christ and given her life to him. She wrote to my friend telling him what had happened. He was completely overwhelmed by the way God had used him.

So often it is when we move beyond our comfort zone and make ourselves available to witness, to go on mission and to do evangelism, that our faith comes alive and we begin to live more fruitfully as disciples of Jesus Christ.

How to lead a person to Christ

I have sometimes been quite shocked to discover that people who have been Christians for many years, who take a leading role in the life of the church (even preaching and teaching), seem completely incapable of leading someone to faith. We never know when this moment will come. I was totally unprepared for it when flying on a British Airways flight to a conference in the Philippines. It seems that the other twenty evangelists on board were in the same position, because when I asked if any of them had a Christian tract or gospel I could give away, not one of them had anything to hand.

The air hostess was looking tired and stressed. As she passed out the dinner trays, I looked up into her eyes and sensed a deep pain there. 'How are you?' I asked.

She paused, looking down at me. 'Are you really interested?' she said.

I nodded.

'Okay, I'll come and tell you after the dinner service is finished.'

She gave out all the meals, then came to sit in the aisle beside me. She told me about how stressed she was, how lonely she felt and how tired she'd become. We began to talk and quickly we travelled up the scale to level five. I went with her to the galley and she made me a cup of coffee. As the conversation continued, she began to talk about faith and her search for God. She explained that her flat-mate had become a Christian and the transformation in her life had been so profound, *she* wanted to find Christ too. But she had never dared ask her friend exactly how it worked. A fellowship group had started to meet in the flat, but she had never been asked to go; so she had retreated to her room, just joining them for coffee at the end of each evening. The groundwork had been laid, the witness of her flat-mate had born fruit, and now she wanted to find Christ for herself. As I had neither tracts nor Bibles to hand, I had to use my little diagrammatic pattern to show how you become a Christian. She prayed with me there and then in the aircraft galley. Two weeks later I met her on the runway at Kuala Lumpur airport, and gave her a Bible and some reading notes to get her started.

Having, perhaps, laboured the point that we should never approach personal evangelism as an opportunity to go through our Christian 'sales patter', I do find it useful to have some kind of structure when I feel that someone is ready to hear and to respond. I'd have been lost without it in the aircraft galley that night! There are many possible ways of describing the process of salvation, and many clever diagrammatic methods have been devised. As I have already said, I certainly wouldn't want to use this outline as a formula for 'cold contact' witnessing, and I certainly wouldn't stick to any rigid script. I would simply sprinkle the key points about salvation through my conversation with the listener.

The nine-point agenda I use in witnessing to non-Christians is an amalgam of several others, and I have adapted it to suit a wide range of situations and listeners over the years. I don't particularly advocate this programme, but I have found it to be a clear presentation of the process of salvation which can be easily understood by all kinds of people.

1. A perfect world

There was a time when the world was perfect, and when humankind and God lived in perfect unity and understanding. God would never have made something that was imperfect. He looked at it and it was good! Creator and created were in relationship.

In the beginning God created the heavens and the earth.

2. A fallen world

The perfection of the created order was stained, smashed and spoiled by humankind's rebellion. Because we were given free will, we had the option to reject God's way and go our own. Because of our selfishness the world has been polluted by sin. What was perfect was made imperfect, and the special relationship that had existed between God and human beings was severed.

> [Jesus said,] 'For from within, out of men's hearts, come evil thoughts, sexual immorality, theft, murder, adultery, greed, malice, deceit, lewdness, envy, slander, arrogance and folly. All these evils come from inside and make a man "unclean".'

3. Sin separates

It's little wonder, then, that God seems far away. The rebellion and sinfulness of which we are a part, and the personal guilt which all of us carry, act as a barrier between us and God, like a cloud hiding the sun.

> But your iniquities have separated
>   you from your God;
> your sins have hidden his face from you,
>   so that he will not hear.

4. All have sinned

Every one of us has to face up to our personal sin and failure. We are not only part of the fallen nature of the world around us, we have personally rejected God's ways by things we have said, thought and done. We may feel that we are 'good' or 'caring' or 'honest', but nevertheless we have failed in God's eyes. It's like in an examination where the pass mark is 50%, and one candidate gets 5% and another 49%; both have still failed. The Bible teaches that every one of us, without exception, has failed to live up to God's standard.

> For all have sinned and fall short of the glory of God.

5. Separation

This guilt and failure leads to our separation from a holy God. Nothing we could invent ourselves will bridge that gap. Philosophy, morality, good works and even religion are not wide enough to span the chasm between ourselves and our Maker. Even obedience to the ten commandments is not enough.

> Therefore, no-one will be declared righteous in his sight by observing the law; rather, through the law we become conscious of sin.

6. The cross

Every man-made solution to this problem of separation from God rests on our initiative, our works, our effort. It is all futile. Meanwhile, God has provided a way for us to know him and be one with him; yet it is not a reward for what we do. Instead, it comes by faith, and faith alone. It is when we recognise that we can't get to God on our own but need to put our trust in him, that we discover the way.

> Jesus answered, 'I am the way and the truth and the life. No-one comes to the Father except through me. If you really knew me, you would know the Father as well.'

7. Redemption

As we allow Jesus Christ to forgive us, change us and renew us, we become new people. We are 'born again' and discover the joy of this new relationship with God through Jesus Christ. As more and more people are redeemed, they affect the world and become part of the redemption of the world, which will be completed at the end of time.

> Therefore, if anyone is in Christ, he is a new creation; the old has gone, the new has come! All this is from God...

8. Christian growth

When we have received Jesus Christ into our lives to save us and redeem us, we begin a journey with him which is life-enriching and life-transforming. We grow as Christians by reading the Bible, praying, witnessing to and serving others, and through fellowship and worship.

> *Bible*: 'All Scripture is God-breathed and is useful for teaching, rebuking, correcting and training in righteousness, so that the man of God may be thoroughly equipped for every good work.'

> *Prayer*: 'But when you pray, go into your room, close the door and pray to your Father, who is unseen. Then your Father, who sees what is done in secret, will reward you.'

> *Witness*: 'Therefore go and make disciples of all nations, baptising them in the name of the Father and of the Son and of the Holy Spirit...'

> *Worship*: 'Yet a time is coming and has now come when the true worshippers will worship the Father in spirit and truth, for they are the kind of worshippers the Father seeks.'

9. Response

I find that many Christians are reticent about bringing the people to whom they are witnessing to faith. They often hesitate at the last hurdle, and feel unworthy or inadequate. Yet when we move to challenge someone directly about their response to Jesus, I believe the Holy Spirit comes to help us in a special way. Time and again in my own witnessing I've been astonished how easy this last stage can be. When you ask, 'Would you like to become a Christian now?', the answer is regularly 'Yes, please!' However, we can never make that response for another: they must do it themselves. It is a door only they can open. I never force a response, and if people want more time to consider their decision I always give it. If their conversion is to be genuine, it must be based on a whole-hearted response, when they feel completely ready.

Ultimately, we can only lead people so far in their journey to Jesus. Logic, discussion and reason can take the enquirer a long way, but ultimately there must be faith – faith not in me nor my religion, but faith in Jesus – the Saviour, the Way, the Truth and the Life:

> 'Here I am! I stand at the door and knock. If anyone hears my voice and opens the door, I will come in and eat with him, and he with me.'

A good starting point for personal evangelism is to attempt to discover the kind of God the other person believes or doesn't believe in. People like to talk about their beliefs, and in a situation of trust and friendship I have found others more than willing to talk about their views on God.

Once, on a mission in Derbyshire, I went with a group of young people on a hike along a beautiful valley known locally as 'Surprise View'. One of the girls in the group said, 'I used to think of God as someone vague and distant, up there on the hill far away while I was in the valley below. But you've helped me to understand that he's not only just up there; he's down here too, and Jesus is walking with me.' If we can enable people to talk about God and to understand how real he is to us, we will have laid an important foundation. The first principle of personal evangelism is to help others discover that God is a person and that we can best come to know what he is like by looking at his Son, Jesus Christ.

I started off my own search for faith by venturing to find out more about the 'vague power' in the universe. As I began to question and debate, I gradually discovered that the more I learnt about Jesus, the more I discovered about God. I still vividly remember kneeling by myself in the woods of a youth camp outside Birmingham and asking Jesus Christ to come into my life. It took me a year of study, discussion and thought to move from my 'vague power' theory to the discovery that I could get to know this 'vague power' through the person of Jesus Christ.

We need to talk a lot about Jesus. The more we talk about him, the more people will want to know. There is such a richness in his personality, they can't help but be intrigued by him. He is vulnerable, serious, funny, compassionate, thoughtful, serene, concerned, serving, humble, caring, rejected, suffering, anguished and broken. When we begin to talk about Jesus, and to remind people that he is God's Son, we are setting before them the biblical view of God rather than the folk myths of the white-bearded old man, the policeman, the 'vague power' or the magician. We prepare the way for them to meet the true God, not the false gods of our secularised society. We are not trying to get them to put ticks by a set of concepts, like the encyclopaedia salesman. We are not inviting them to give assent to a doctrinal code, like those representing the sects. We are all about introducing people to a friend – Jesus Christ.

One of the darkest pastoral experiences of my whole ministry occurred just a few weeks after I took over my first church. I was summoned to a prison in Wakefield to hear a distraught man confess to murder. He had refused to speak to the police unless there was a 'priest' present, and his statement would be in the form of a confession. Having heard about me in the local newspaper, he chose me to be his 'priest'.

At my interview with him in the top security section of the prison, two murder-squad detectives sat behind me taking notes. It was a bizarre and difficult experience. This intense moment of confession was the start of a friendship with this man which continued for years afterwards. He was torn apart by guilt and beside himself with regret. Gradually, however, as the months went by, I was able to talk to him about Jesus. The more he understood about Jesus, the more he began to recognise that Jesus could be a friend, even to him.

Bible references: John 4:1–26; Luke 19:1–10; Mark 7:21–23; Isaiah 59:2; Romans 3:20,23; John 14:6–7; 2 Corinthians 5:17–18; 2 Timothy 3:16–17; Matthew 6:6; 28:19; John 4:23; Revelation 3:20.

PART 2
Church-based Evangelism

Chapter 5

PRINCIPLES OF CHURCH-BASED EVANGELISM

The churches of the United Kingdom need to stop anticipating decline and start planning for growth. It is time they moved from maintenance to mission and put church-based evangelism at the top of the agenda.

The church exists by mission in the same way that a fire exists by burning. John Skoglund argued that mission is the hallmark of any genuine church. He concluded that the great commission isn't one activity among many but the church's most essential activity. Lesslie Newbigin went further, suggesting that a church which has lost its missionary vision is not an authentic New Testament church. Evangelism is one of the church's core tasks, and the local church is the most appropriate place through which it should be done. Sadly, many churches have lost their vision for this work and don't commit any resources to doing it.

A hospital combines a number of functions. It is a hotel where people are housed; a restaurant where meals are served; a business office where records, accounts, flow charts and job descriptions are kept. Above all else, however, a hospital is a place where people are healed – this is its essential activity. In the same way, the church does many things but its essential activity should be to lead people to Christ. All its other functions should always be secondary. Sadly, many churches don't seem to operate in this way.

A Bible Society research project in 1994 attempted to discover just how committed churches were to the task of evangelism. A representative sample of 400 Protestant ministers and church leaders in England and Wales was selected for the survey, and 203 responses were received. Of the total replies received, a staggering 65% admitted that evangelism was not high on their agenda, and 67% did not accept that the primary purpose of the church was to share the good news of Jesus Christ. Even more disturbing, over half of the sample admitted that they didn't have a regular ongoing programme of evangelism, and over half stated that their congregation would be uncomfortable with such a programme. Almost 70% revealed there was no regular training in evangelism for their congregations. The compilers of the survey used the responses to estimate the relationship between mission and maintenance in churches. They concluded that only one-third of the sample group was 'mission orientated'.

In a detailed assessment of growing Baptist churches around the United Kingdom, Paul Beasley-Murray and Alan Wilkinson observed that many of them were engaged in ongoing programmes of outreach and evangelism. They concluded:

> Growing churches seem to be predominantly those that are expecting great things from God and have that conviction underlying all their activity. Church growth is not simply doing the right things at the right time. It is also a matter of being a fellowship which believes that it is God's plan for His church to grow and having that conviction that He wants it to happen in that particular church: it becomes a matter of faith.

I believe there is a huge resource of committed Christians waiting to be released into dynamic evangelistic outreach. We need to learn how to mobilise them, give them skills to reach the emerging generation, and show them how to use the local church as their base. If they are to be effective, they need to grasp the following basic principles of church-based evangelism.

Church-based evangelism must be incarnational

Some Christians commute several miles to church, park their cars in the car park and attend worship. Immediately after the service, they get back into their cars and drive several miles home again. Unfortunately, they have no mid-week contact with the neighbourhood which forms the context for their church's mission. Churches consisting of commuter Christians like these can't do evangelism properly. If a church is to be effective evangelistically, it must relate to the community in which it is set, and its congregation must constantly be building networks of relationship, service and witness within their locality. A church cut off from its community is like a tree cut off from its roots – it is weak and barren!

Jesus' identification with humanity was complete. By his birth he 'became flesh and made his dwelling among us'; in his life he was 'numbered with the transgressors'; in his death he 'bore our sins in his body'. He 'shared in [our] humanity so that by his death he might destroy him who holds the power of death'. And he made his incarnation the model for the church's mission. He told his disciples, 'As the Father has sent me, I am sending you.' The former bishop of Liverpool, David Sheppard, has commented, 'If we can believe God is really incarnate He is frighteningly close, and He meets us where we are. The followers of Jesus have to live in that world too: like Him we are called to meet people where they are.'

Church history is full of examples of Christians who have been willing to accept this painful model of incarnation as their method of mission. Throughout his ministry we see the apostle Paul becoming 'incarnate' within the communities of various groups of people. At Philippi he spoke with Lydia and the other women by the riverbank, and shared a cell with the prisoners in a Philippian jail. In Athens he debated with Jews and Greeks in the synagogue and the marketplace, and argued with Epicurean and Stoic philosophers. Paul's method of evangelism was all about meeting people where they were, relating to them in their own context, and presenting the gospel in ways that were relevant to their felt needs and aspirations – incarnational evangelism at its best.

Another good example is the famous nineteenth-century missionary to China, James Hudson Taylor. He adopted Chinese dress and customs, and mingled freely with the Chinese people. It was a revolutionary style of working for his time:

> A belief in the equality of all men before God, too literally acted upon, can produce patterns of behaviour which no imperial society can accept with equanimity. To the Taipans and all the other people who believed that the white man's dignity rested in strict adherence to British dress and habits Hudson Taylor's action was deeply shocking. He had gone 'native'. He had lost face. He had broken the magic ring of white solidarity. *(George Woodcock)*

Just as Hudson Taylor needed to shed his cultural trappings to become a living witness in Chinese society, so we as Christians must be willing to ditch much of our middle-class subculture if we are to become incarnate in contemporary society. However, this does not mean that we lose our identity. In becoming one of us Jesus did not cease to be himself.

Church-based evangelism must reach the unreached

Many congregations who think they are 'doing evangelism' are in fact just talking to themselves. Their glossy handouts never get beyond the fringes of the fellowship, their guest services only bring in the 'lapsed', and their sermons only preach to the converted. It takes great commitment and determination for a church to 'reach the unreached'.

Evangelism to people who have never heard the true Christian message should be the highest priority for every church in the world. Sadly, many have turned their back on those who have never heard the good news. When scholar

Rupert Davies examined the role of evangelism in the Methodist Church, he concluded: 'It has, of course, not disowned the narrower and more intense forms of evangelism, but it has tended to leave them to certain vigorous groups within itself and often, too often, to evangelists from overseas.' Yet Methodism's founder, John Wesley, instructed his helpers that they 'go always, not only to those who need you, but to those who need you most'. If we are to engage in effective evangelism, then, we must be willing to move beyond the friendship networks of our fellowship and identify the 'unreached people-groups' around us.

In traditional church life, we expect people first to behave; then to believe; then to belong. But Jesus did not adopt this approach in his ministry. He first welcomed people so that they belonged; then they could learn how to behave, after which they believed. We see him do this with Matthew, for example, who moved from being a tax collector – a job which put him in the category of 'sinner and social pariah' as far as the society of his day was concerned – to becoming one of Jesus' band of disciples, an apostle and, eventually, the author of one of the Gospels:

> As Jesus went on from there, he saw a man named Matthew sitting at the tax collector's booth. 'Follow me,' he told him, and Matthew got up and followed him...
>
> He called his twelve disciples to him and gave them authority to drive out evil spirits and to heal every disease and sickness.
> These are the names of the twelve apostles: first, Simon ... Thomas and Matthew the tax collector; James...

Matthew was first invited to belong; as he sat with the other disciples and heard Jesus' teaching, he learned what following Jesus was all about; then he believed. Personally, I am convinced this is the right model for church evangelism. Rather than treating them like outsiders and second-class citizens, the first step we should take is to encourage people to belong by accepting them into our community and inviting them to journey with us. As they become part of us, they learn what Christians believe and how we should behave as citizens of God's kingdom. Then, as they see the difference faith is making in our lives, they can decide whether or not they want to share in our beliefs.

Church-based evangelism must be culturally relevant

Christians need to learn the language of those who cannot understand our religious terminology. Too often we are answering questions people are not asking and speaking in ways that put them off. Sadly, many churches are so middle-class in their language, dress, culture and thinking, they seem unapproachable to those from working-class or other backgrounds:

> This is a class-ridden nation, and the Christian faith has become a middle class religion. In practice it often seems irrelevant to the working person. We need to free our faith from its cultural entrapment. *(Clive Calver)*

Those wanting to engage in church-based evangelism need to understand their target audience and how to communicate in ways they will hear and understand. In recent surveys, it was determined that about 23% of non-churchgoers don't read a newspaper, and about 22% of the population never read a book. The language of film, music, drama and dance is the vernacular of many and is the language used by the contemporary media and modern advertising, which doesn't so much appeal to linear thinking as to 'gut reactions' and which uses images as much as words. What you experience is as important as what you read, maybe more so. If the local church is offering forms of worship that are too cerebral, its message won't get through. Local church life and outreach must be seen to work and to be directly relevant to people's lives.

Church-based evangelism must be spiritual

Many people in society today still have a religious framework for their lives even though they live outside the orbit of their local church. They have a basic understanding of spirituality, and most can distinguish between what is real and what is sham. In a recent religious survey among 1,500 adults, researchers discovered that:

76% believed in God
68% believed in a soul
49% believed in life after death
69% believed in sin
31% believed in hell
4% were atheists
4% were agnostics

Even in this highly secularised society, it seems, people still have an understanding of basic Christian teaching. Many of them express a deep longing for love, for transcendence and identity. Those in their twenties, thirties and forties are exploring new forms of popular spirituality. This exploration is one of the most significant characteristics of new millennium society. Thousands of ordinary people continue their inward journey of discovery in weekly Yoga classes, T'ai Chi groups, meditation sessions, aromatherapy clinics and occult covens in communities all over the country. The growth of phenomena such as New Age thinking, star signs, meditation and alternative medicine is offering a plethora of new religious perspectives. A Gallup survey among British teenagers in the mid-1980s revealed that over 50% of them said they believed astrology worked in some form. Nicci Gerrard, writing in the *Observer*, observed our contemporary addiction to fate:

> We 'fall' in love. Then out again. It's not our fault. Madness
> 'descends'. Meetings are 'meant'. Things 'turn out' for the best
> or 'just happen'. It's a 'foregone conclusion'. It was 'in the stars'.
> We grasp at coincidences.

This plurality of meaning is the driving force behind secularism and runs contrary to the Christian gospel. Urban men and women 'pick and mix' their religious beliefs from a bewildering display in the supermarket of life.

Recently, I crossed the threshold of a New Age shop in a small Devon town. I hoped none of my evangelical Christian friends would think I'd lost my senses as I browsed the bookshelves and eavesdropped on conversations by the health-food display cabinet. Customers in the shop, which was one of several in the high street, were buying books on meditation, tapes for relaxation, and homeopathic and health-food products. Their search for spirituality had become part of the Saturday shopping ritual, sandwiched somewhere between Boots and Sainsbury's. The New Age shop was one of the busiest in the High Street. Spiritual things were discussed freely and there was an openness to anyone seeking a spiritual perspective on life. I wondered if there was more talk of the spiritual disciplines here than in the church directly opposite. All it advertised was an autumn bazaar and a holiday slide show.

Hunger for the spiritual has gone mainstream, and this trend will grow rapidly beyond 2000. The search for meaning is on. The eminent psychologist Carl Gustav Jung observed, 'Among all my patients in the second half of their life [age 35+] ... there has not been one whose problem in the last resort was not that of finding a religious outlook on life.' We disregard the spiritual side of our existence at our peril. Sociologists tell us that the modernist era has ignored the spiritual dimension of our humanity in favour of scientific method. Postmodernism, however, will reaffirm the importance of the mystical and the spiritual.

Those of us committed to evangelism must face up to the challenge as to how we can start a meaningful dialogue with the world and demonstrate the power of God for all to see. The debate about explanation and meaning rolls ever onward. The question is, how can we, as contemporary Christians, enter into it? More importantly, have we something meaningful to say to a world fascinated by religious questions but disinterested in traditional answers? How can we challenge the existentialist view that 'what is spiritual truth for you is true and what is spiritual truth for me is true, and I accept that your spiritual truth is as true as my own'? I find increasingly that people are disinterested in talk about church, theology or doctrine. The question they are asking is, 'Does Christianity work for you?' We need to demonstrate that it really does and, what's more, it can work for them as well.

Church-based evangelism must use preaching

The art of preaching is making a come-back. Not on Presbyterian platforms or in cathedral pulpits, but in West End theatres, luxurious conference suites, five-star banqueting halls, city libraries and dark smoky bars. Thousands queue for a ticket to hear Ben Elton, Billy Connolly or John Gray preach their various versions of the secular gospel on West End stages – two-hour sermons, with ice creams in the interval. Corporate executives pay upwards of £100 a ticket to hear management gurus like Charles Handy expound their latest business theories spiced with humorous personal experiences. Retired politicians, pop stars, authors, newsreaders and sports personalities make a healthy living on the 'speaking circuit', delivering personal anecdotes over fine wine and good cigars. In libraries and school halls up and down the UK, a new generation of public speakers are making a living by telling stories. The growth of the comedy-club circuit has been astronomic in recent years, giving a wonderful new opportunity for radical young comedians to rehearse 40-minute routines based largely on anecdotal stories. Believe it or not, 'preaching' (one person talking to a lot of other people) is popular once again.

As usual, some local churches are the last to catch on. We are still in the 'Can you keep it short, please, pastor?' mode and the '*Must* we have a sermon, vicar?' syndrome. Everywhere I go, I hear that church leaders are lengthening the worship, replacing the sermon with 'discussion groups', filling the church with fancy visual aids and suggesting that preaching is inappropriate for today. The ministry of preaching is going through a lean time.

There is a feeling in some churches that the era of evangelistic preaching is dead. I have heard it said that it is inappropriate to our culture and incongruous for our time. But it's time we recognised that the evangelistic sermon is one of the most compelling means of communication known to humankind. History should remind us that God speaks through the preached word and a human heart on fire for him. I personally believe that preaching *is* a relevant method of communication and the church should rescue it from the rubbish heap of ecclesiastical has-beens before it's too late! A good preacher's life experiences and personality are the greatest visual aids we can ever use. They will always be relevant because a preacher who has been listening to her audience carefully is actually engaging in a conversation with them, but it's just her turn to speak.

Recently, I was at a conference of around seventy young preachers. They were from a diverse denominational background and many of them were in their twenties. I've been hearing their pain, sensing their frustration, seeing the wasted opportunity of gifts unused. Many of them have never been affirmed by their pastor, never been given an opportunity to test their call, never had helpful sermon crits, let alone been given basic skills in the craft of evangelistic sermon-making. Many church leaders have chosen to go with the flow, let the worship speak and get trendy with the big-screen video and sound-bite messages. In so doing they have lost the greatest means of communication God ever gave to the church – the preacher! We have gagged the emerging generation of evangelistic preachers whom God has called for us. The gospel messages God is giving them go unheard, and the anointing he has poured out on them is going down the drain.

For more than a generation, the evangelistic preacher has had a bad deal. He has been mocked by the media, misunderstood by the world and marginalised by the church. There are endless courses, conferences and consultations on the role of the worship leader, but evangelistic preaching remains the Cinderella ministry of the contemporary church. I personally believe that it's time for evangelistic preaching to make a come-back in the church!

Church-based evangelism must relate to gender

Recently, I was given two press tickets to a lecture. I must say that I wouldn't normally want to spend the whole of a Friday evening at a lecture, but this was quite an event! It was a two-and-a-half hour 'sermon' delivered by John Gray, the author of one of the most popular books on the planet, *Men are from Mars, Women are from Venus*. Several hundred well-dressed professionals crowded into the theatre, each having paid between £25 and £45 per ticket, while my wife and I were ushered into a private bar to meet Mr Gray and to mingle with the media glitterati.

Throughout his lecture, Gray talked in spiritual terms. Some of the spiritual language he used would be recognisable in any church setting. Yet I felt uneasy. At the end of the presentation I plucked up the courage to ask Gray's press agent directly, 'Is this spirituality he's advocating Christian?' The tall gentleman beamed at me. 'No way,' he said. 'John gets his inspiration from the East.' He went on to explain that John would be giving more attention to Eastern meditation techniques in his next seminar, which would be entitled 'How to get what you want'.

One of the most popular gurus on the twenty-something scene is not a Christian, and his teaching stems from a philosophy vastly different to that of Jesus Christ. It's a religion of self-help rather than God-help. And there's a lot of common sense in what he teaches.

Gray's mission is to help individuals recognise that their partner comes from a 'different planet'. Once this has been appreciated, they can relax and co-operate with the differences instead of resisting or trying to change them. He points out that, for example, most women like to talk about their day, while most men don't. Women like to watch TV programmes in their entirety; men prefer to surf with the remote control. Tidiness is important to a woman; it's not so crucial for a man. Younger men are sexually aroused quickly; women more slowly. Men like to solve problems while women prefer to discuss them. Women don't like to ask men for emotional support; men don't offer it instinctively – they like to be asked! Gray has now set up an organization in the UK called 'Mars–Venus Workshops', which aims to help corporations and industries in facilitating a greater understanding between the sexes at work. The demand for these is incredible. I talked at length to two of the workshop leaders who expressed the hope that by helping men and women through their differences they can improve teamwork, efficiency and communication.

After years of counselling people with relationship problems, Gray has evidently stumbled on some very practical advice. (To be fair, he did admit that he was generalising and there were plenty of exceptions to every principle. However, there was a lot of truth in what he taught, and I'm sure that many returned home feeling that their £45 was money well spent.) It is evident to anyone who mixes with the opposite sex that men *are* very different from women. Whether this is biological or cultural is irrelevant, we know that these differences exist. Local church-based evangelism must begin to understand them and to address the fact that women think, relate and make decisions in very different ways from men.

I personally advocate all-male and all-female meetings as part of local church-based evangelism. I'm convinced that we need to learn how to present the gospel to men and women in different ways, and how to take gender into account. 'Colour me beautiful' programmes for women, for example, have been effective and popular. An expert in skin-tone and fashion lectured over a hundred suburban women at a local church mission I was leading near Sheffield, and demonstrated the importance of colour co-ordination, poise and style. Her excellent talk led to a personal testimony about inner wholeness which spoke of Christ's transforming power in her own life. Meanwhile, a group of men were meeting in a local pub to discuss 'Stress at Work'. A trained leader helped them to identify the pressures they were facing and taught how prayer and Christian meditation could help.

Much work needs to be done on the concept of gender in evangelism. We must learn much more about how men and women think, respond and make decisions if we want to be truly effective. What better way is there to ensure that this is done than by having male and female evangelists on every team! Sadly, as in many aspects of the church's mission, women are under-represented in the ministry of evangelism. Many churches still see the role of evangelist as exclusively male. I would like to see more women called to and affirmed in the work. One thing is for sure, one of the most effective evangelists Jesus encountered during his ministry was the woman from Samaria: many people from her town came to believe because of her testimony!

Church-based evangelism must be sensitive to personality

There are all sorts of 'indicators' and theories around today regarding defining personality types, such as the Enneagram, and Situationism (advocated by Walter Mischel). The Myers-Briggs Type indicator was developed by Katherine Briggs and her daughter.

Briggs was fascinated by the similarities and differences between people and began to develop lists of characteristics. Just after the Second World War she discovered that psychologist Carl Jung had developed a similar system, so she began to adopt his 'theory of types'. Jung's primary distinction was between extrovert and introvert types. He suggested that extroverts prefer to focus on the outer world of things and people, and draw their energy from there. Introverts, however, prefer to focus on the inner world of ideas and concepts, and draw their energy from there. This kind of analysis makes a lot of sense. We all know people who are more bubbly and outgoing or who are more quiet and reserved. This, however, is only the beginning of the Myers-Briggs Indicator!

I recently went on a three-day Myers-Briggs course and found it most challenging. Through lectures and question-naires, the tutor led ten of us intrepid personality explorers through two ways of perceiving (sensing and intuiting), two ways of making decisions (thinking and feeling), and two ways of living (judging and perceiving), until most of us in the group could clearly see which 'type' most described us. I sighed with relief as I began to discover myself clearly described in the descriptions of my personality type. It made me recognise where my weaknesses are and why I have cho-sen so many people who are better at organising minutiae, making decisions and being logical to work in my team. They are there to complement me in my weaknesses!

As the course continued, however, I began to realise how obvious it was that these theories have an important applica-tion in the evangelistic outreach of the church. Who do many churches appoint to welcome newcomers at the door, for example? The most extrovert member of the congregation! But what does that do to an introvert attending church for the first time? It frightens them away for ever! An introvert would much prefer no welcome at all, but a notice board beside which to hang around, some personal space and the opportunity to meet people in a non-threatening way at their own speed and pace.

I then began to reflect on the different styles of church evangelism I have engaged in over the years, and how some of them must have been deeply threatening to people of cer-tain personality types. As someone who has been a 'travelling evangelist' for nearly twenty years, I can see clearly now that many of the styles of evangelism I have engaged in have probably appealed more to extroverts like myself, and there has been a dearth of effective evangelism among introverts.

Myers-Briggs is only a theory, and pushed to the limit I'm

pretty sure it's a theory that might break down. It does, how-ever, remind all of us in church life of one very important fact: people are different. If we use the wrong styles of evan-gelism on the wrong people, we may alienate or even damage them. A football stadium and an opportunity to step out publicly in front of 50,000 onlookers may appeal to some but will scare the living daylights out of others. A gentle, friendly 'Alpha' group which meets the needs of some may be a hellish ordeal for others. We need to learn how to get alongside different people in different ways just as Jesus did. One thing's for sure, however – he is calling us all to follow him, no matter what personality type we have.

Bible references: John 1:14; Isaiah 53:12; 1 Peter 2:24; Hebrews 2:14; John 20:21; Acts 16:11–40; 17:16–34; 1 Corinthians 9:19–22; Matthew 9:9; 10:1–2; John 4:39.

Book references: Paul Beasley-Murray and Alan Wilkinson, *Turning the Tide*, The Bible Society, 1990; David Sheppard, *Bias to the Poor*, Hodder and Stoughton, 1983; George Woodcock, *The British in the Far East*; Rupert Davies, *Testing of the Churches*, Epworth Press; Clive Calver, *The Truth About Truth*, Monarch, 1997.

Chapter 6

PREPARATIONS FOR LOCAL CHURCH EVANGELISM

In chapter one I described one of the first missions I ever led, at the beach resort of Newquay in Cornwall. It was great fun! Every day scores of children and young teenagers gathered on the beach for stories and games, and we really enjoyed getting to know them.

As the days went by, some of these kids wanted to know more about Jesus, and members of our team had the privilege of leading several of them to Christ. We were overjoyed but soon realised we had no effective way of following them up. Within a couple of days they would return home and our team would be dispersed throughout the country. We began to phone round our contacts in the areas where these young people lived. However, it became clear how difficult it was to introduce a stranger to a church they knew nothing about and where nobody knew them.

There was an enormous sense of frustration at not being able to follow up these young converts, but through it I learned an important lesson – the best base for evangelism is not a holiday beach but a local church. The most effective team for witness and follow-up in a community isn't a disparate team who are here today and gone tomorrow, but a group of local Christians who live their lives as though they are always 'on mission'.

In many towns and cities, God's greatest tool for evangelism – the church – has become a blunt instrument. Congregations don't recognise the crucial importance of this outreach ministry and follow an agenda which is more about servicing the flock than searching for lost sheep. Here and there I am encouraged to see that some churches are waking up to the task and rediscovering the vital role they can play in the evangelisation of their area. If every local church was functioning evangelistically, there would be a natural link between its ongoing witness in the community, its outreach through sharing the faith, and its nurture of new Christians. Every church should function like a mission team! The local church is the God-ordained unit for mission and it's time that each fellowship developed a sense of responsibility for evangelism in their area. The motivation shouldn't be to 'get extra members' but to fulfil Christ's commission to 'go into all the world and preach the gospel'.

Over the last fifteen years Share Jesus teams in different parts of the world have worked with hundreds of churches to help them evangelise their neighbourhoods. Although the actual mission may take only a week, the work of preparation begins months beforehand. Time and again, local ministers say that this process of preparing has been invaluable. Many churches actually rediscover their evangelistic ministry long before the week of mission begins.

The seven processes we facilitate in the run-up to a Share Jesus mission are listed below. My hope is that they may be adapted and modified for local situations in any part of the world!

1. Praying for the church

Several years ago a Korean minister arrived at our church in Raynes Park and asked if he could rent a room. Our premises are fairly well used, but when he explained that he needed the room from five until eight in the morning, there didn't seem much of a problem!

As I arrived at my office a few days later, I stopped in amazement. Echoing down the stairwell was the voice of this stranger, crying out to God in the Korean language for our church and for the people of Raynes Park. As I got to know him better, he explained that there could be no revival without prayer. He believed that prayer is the key to fruitfulness in the kingdom of God. I felt humbled and convicted by this stranger's commitment to pray for a neighbourhood and a church so far from his home.

I'm convinced that church mission without commitment to prayer is largely a waste of time. Prayer is the single most important factor in moving a church to mission. I know that when I pray for my own church and community, something significant happens in me! I begin to view the whole concept of mission in a different way. When I prayer-walked the streets near my home in Raynes Park, I began to sense the spiritual need of those who lived around me as never before. When I prayed with a small group of friends for my neighbours and acquaintances, I focused on their need for Christ as never before. When I joined with a local congregation to cry out to God deep into the night for the needs of our area, I sensed his blessing in special ways.

Prayer is the fuel for mission. When the prayer dries up, the mission usually splutters to a halt. Those engaging in mission must be reliant on prayer, and they must see prayer as the key to their effectiveness. Something happens in a fellowship when people pray: God begins to work in significant ways. Any church which wants to engage in mission must get serious about prayer. It prepares the ground for mission and the people to hear the good news about Jesus.

2. Believing in growth

When a church is in decline, it can be demoralising for everyone involved. For many years I only ever seemed to attend church meetings in which decline and retrenchment were featured. The conversation centred on such questions as 'Shall we close this church, withdraw the minister, cease the work?' This kind of defensive thinking can have a deeply disturbing effect on church life. Many congregations don't seem to believe that it's possible for their church to grow. Some find it incredible that 'in this day and age' people can come to faith in Jesus! However, there are many books and resources on church growth, and I would encourage church leaders to study them. While many struggle with any kind of 'formula' for growth, I am sure there are principles we can all learn and understand.

Strategists tell us that there are a variety of ways in which a church can grow. First, there is internal growth in which Christians within a church become better disciples. This is essentially growth in quality rather than quantity, but it may mean that some people within the life of the church become committed Christians. We must never forget to evangelise within the church as well as outside it!

Second, there is the kind of growth that involves expansion, when a church decides to get out among the unchurched in its community and win them for Christ; these new disciples are then nurtured in the context of the church. Many missions and guest services work on this principle, and it continues to be very effective. Every church should see this as part of their ongoing programme of activities.

Then there is the growth that happens when a church identifies a specific group of people who have no Christian witness among them. Reaching such a group will probably mean that church members have to go to live and work among them. Through being present, through their service and witness, it's likely that some will become Christians and be linked with the fellowship. This kind of mission is generally considered to be the most effective evangelistic method of all. Many of Britain's most successful house-churches have used this model extensively.

Finally, but most difficult of all, there's the growth that occurs when a church seeks to start a new church in a culture different from its own. This will involve pioneer church-planters becoming completely enculturalised in a different community from the one they are used to.

If we are to prepare a local church for mission, then we must create a faith context in which men and women are believing that their church can grow, asking God for growth and expecting growth to happen. Without this theological and spiritual base, all mission will seem like a set of programmes rather than a strategy for helping the church to grow. The aim is to create an atmosphere in which there is a continuous drive towards growth.

3. Asking painful questions

As part of the move to encourage prayer and build faith, church leaders might find it helpful to undertake a comprehensive survey of their church's life and ministry. This isn't easy, and it's important that everyone takes part and looks at the process positively and constructively.

Counting the flock

Gibbs, Pointer and McGavran – three of the world's leading church-growth experts – all agree that churches should regularly count their attendees, community roll and membership to ascertain where there is decline and where there is growth. These experts believe that detailed surveys of churches should also be undertaken to check their spiritual health. McGavran uses the example of a nurse using a thermometer to assess the patient's temperature: the thermometer will not help the patient get better, but it is a tool to help diagnose the his or her condition. In the same way, church growth surveys don't help the church to grow, but they give an assessment so that an intelligent diagnosis can be made.

McGavran defends in particular the activity of counting people and working with numbers. He argues that because the church is made up of countable people, there is nothing particularly spiritual in not counting them. The numerical approach is used in all kinds of human endeavour, including industry, commerce, finance, research, government and invention: much of human enterprise is developed by continual measurement.

As the trends of growth and decline in a church are identified and tabulated, the information can be studied and discussed by everyone involved in order to determine what has been happening in the life of their church.

Plotting where people live

The next task is to plot the location of the church membership on a large map of the area. At Share Jesus we do this
with many of the churches we work with, and the results are
often startling. It is surprising how many have never undertaken such a simple exercise. Time and again, when I've done
this with church groups, we have discovered that church
members live in one area of town or in clusters around the
neighbourhood, but quite often don't live near the church.
Indeed, I've worked with some churches which have hardly
any members living in their immediate catchment area at all!

When I begin to ask questions about these 'clusters', I
sometimes discover that the members all come from one
social milieu. I came across a startling example of this in a
small town in Bedfordshire. When the leaders plotted their
church membership, they discovered that every one of them
lived on the chapel side of a main road. This was the 'old village' community, which tended to be more middle-class.
There wasn't a single member living on the large council over-
spill estate on the other side of the road. The main road
marked a gulf between two communities and the folk on the
other side of the road were an 'unreached people-group' as far
as the church was concerned. This church's mission audit led
them to recognise their own exclusiveness, their lack of witness among a needy group of people living close by, and their
ineffectiveness in reaching the young people in their neighbourhood. It led to the planting of a new work 'across the
road', beginning in the school and the workingmen's club,
and leading to evangelistic house groups in various homes.

Part of a church mission audit is to identify people-groups,
blocks of housing, streets or neighbourhoods where there is
little or no Christian witness. These could well be rich seams
for the gospel if there is effective evangelism among them.

Telling the church's story

Every church has a history – a history of success and failure,
growth and decline, good times and bad. If a church is to

engage in effective mission, it is important that this story is told. Our mission teams have developed a questionnaire on this, for use in local churches, which serves as a trigger for discussion (it is included in Appendix 1 at the end of this book). We often find that as the church members fill in the questionnaire, the discussion it generates is often valuable as an exercise in itself. It enables people to talk about their church, and to review the groups within it and the church's life generally. They can also explore the church's relationship with the community in which it is set. When a church begins to ask fundamental questions like 'What are we trying to do?', 'How effective are we?' and 'Where are we headed?', this provides a natural forum in which mission and evangelism can be discussed and initiated. The questionnaire is designed to help church members face facts and get real with each other. Too many of them live in a kind of 'sanctified escapism' in which hard questions are not faced and difficult decisions not made.

Every church should regularly review its life and ask hard questions about its effectiveness in reaching the local community. Every church should constantly be assessing its neighbourhood, and discovering fresh ways of interacting with it and communicating to it the truth about Jesus.

Looking inward, looking outward

The next task is to assess a church's effectiveness in evangelism. One of the quickest ways of doing this is to ask the various groups in the life of a church – from the women's fellowship to the Boys' Brigade, from mother-and-baby groups to mid-week Bible-study meetings – to undertake a period of self-assessment and to look at the way in which they welcome newcomers. When our mission teams undertake this task in a church, we often invite each organisation to score its effectiveness as an agent for outreach in the church's life, and then to look at its pattern of growth or decline over recent years. Their leaders are invited to help them by asking searching questions. Who has joined? Why have they joined? How has belonging helped them in their pilgrimage of faith?

The responses to these questions must be handled compassionately and with care. There should be no sense of competition or comparison between different groups but, rather, an attempt by all of them to identify ways of developing their effectiveness in evangelism. Those that take the findings seriously are sometimes disturbed or even devastated by the results of these surveys. I have known some completely revamp their programmes so that they have a greater interface with the local community or a more prominent evangelistic emphasis.

Preparing a report

The collation of all this information should give church leaders a broad idea of their congregation's effectiveness in mission. Findings about the church's strengths and weaknesses need to be thought through and addressed. It is sometimes helpful to bring in an outside consultant to help leaders 'articulate the story' to the congregation. They may be too close to what's happening to unpack it creatively and look at it in the cold light of reason. The story may be about growth, decline, secession, division, failure, success, tradition, institution or pain. Telling this story can be therapeutic in itself, and healing can result if the process is handled well. Sometimes churches can't move on in mission until they have resolved aspects of their history which hold them back.

Growing dissatisfied

Church mission audits can facilitate evangelism by creating a 'holy unease' which jump-starts a membership out of despondency, helps them to see decline as unacceptable and moves them on to begin local outreach. Corporate executives of the world's most successful industries are taught this 'restless dissatisfaction' as a management tool. It is a healthy state of mind which drives the company forward to become more efficient and to identify new markets. Whenever I read the book of Acts, I sense a similar hunger for growth – a thirst for development, a vision for the future. The apostles were good at forecasting, and people like Paul expressed a holy unease which compelled them to reach out to new mission fields.

The process of auditing should create a feeling of dissatisfaction with who we are, what we do and how we function. This dissatisfaction is the key to mobilising a church into mission and evangelism. Where a church fellowship remains smug and complacent, it won't see the need for evangelism or glimpse a vision for the world.

A church audit can sometimes prompt churches to work more closely with other groups of Christians in their area. I am sure that where churches work together in mission, God blesses in special ways. Different fellowships have different gifts and strengths, and they may be more effective in winning people for Christ if they work in partnership with others.

4. Understanding your community

Having audited the life of the local congregation, the next step is to look at the context in which the church is set and to assess how best to do evangelism within it. When missionaries go to foreign fields, they often spend months looking at the cultural, sociological, religious and economic profiles of the group with whom they are working. Rarely, if ever, do local church congregations undertake a similar discipline when looking at the context for their evangelism! It's little wonder, then, that we are often saying the wrong things at the wrong time to the wrong people. A few hours of research in the local library, or among the housing and employment statistics in the local council record office, can be very revealing. It is sometimes even possible to purchase a demographic and socio-economic survey of an area from the council.

One of the best ways to engage a congregation in confronting the needs and possibilities of its catchment area is to get *them* to do the survey. There are a wide range of basic formats for doing this on offer from different mission agencies. The one we use in Share Jesus seeks to gain a deeper understanding of the nature of a community, its strengths, weaknesses and friendliness. (A sample is included in Appendix 2. In conducting the survey, we generally train our interviewers to introduce themselves as coming from the local church which is trying to discover ways of serving their community more effectively.) When church members carry out this survey, they begin to understand better the felt needs of people in the neighbourhood instead of relying on their own, often outdated assumptions. The aim is not to provide opportunities for personal evangelism, but to give Christians a feel for the mission field around them.

Some years ago I was working with a congregation which was deeply concerned about its lack of children's outreach, Sunday school meetings and kids' clubs. Years before they had been well-known for their Sunday school, which had numbered hundreds of attendees. When they completed their community survey they discovered, to their amazement, that there were hardly any children living in the area! The population had aged, the children had grown up and moved away – even the local school was threatened with closure. Their research helped them to recognise that children's work was inappropriate for their context. So instead they invested time and energy in developing effective programmes of outreach for the elderly and the housebound. A similar survey carried out ten years later might well reveal that the estate was filling up with young couples and the area repopulating with children again! Community surveys, then, are not a 'once in a lifetime' activity for a church: they should be done again and again across the years.

The community survey helps to identify who is living around the church, but also, more importantly, how they feel about the area and what they are looking for. When the congregation bridges the gap between what they think people need and what they actually want, the church will become much more effective in mission and evangelism.

5. Welcoming the world

Surveys can also help to identify people-groups living in an area. There was a time in church mission when you could look at the geographical 'parish' in which the church was set, and seek ways of reaching that defined area and population for Christ. In the village life of previous centuries the whole community network seemed to revolve around church, pub and shop.

Today the large metropolitan areas which make up the United Kingdom are vastly different. Where I live in south-west London it is hard to find any geographical boundaries between the different boroughs. Sociologists tell us that people who live in these great cities do not have a 'geographical' view of the community in which they live. Their relationships are based around places of work, leisure, the school, the club, the pub, the hobby-group and the learning centre. Evangelism in this context should be less about trying to reach the entire population of a geographical area and more about witnessing to the different people-groups:

> [C]ultures develop in communities which are distinctive from their neighbours and are held together by patterns of economic and social cooperation reinforced by custom, language, tradition, history and networks of moral interdependence and reciprocity. As these are established and sedimented over time they lead to customary understandings and obligations, patterns of expectations that do not require to be calculated or defended. *(Peter Anthony)*

The churches of the new millennium need to witness within these cultures and to absorb their characteristics if they are to be relevant and welcoming.

There are a number of people-groups with whom the church seems to have little or no contact. According to MARC Europe (*Christian England*, 1991), one of those groups is 'young marrieds': while churches seem able to contact parents with young children, they do particularly badly with those who are 'just married'. Churches are also renowned for their inability to work with men: women are much more predominant in church life. Ethnic minority groups are largely absent, particularly those from an Asian culture. Other people-groups difficult to contact are teenagers and those who are separated and divorced. Church members also tend to be more 'upper-class' than the average sociological profile in any given area.

One of the best ways to reach a people-group is to develop personal relationships with the people in them and then to form a cell group. (The Vineyard church calls these 'kinship groups'; the house church Ichthus calls them 'neighbourhood groups'; Pioneer churches label them 'home church'. Other more established churches are using the 'Alpha group' concept established by Holy Trinity, Brompton, to reach specific people-groups.) This cell group is basically a church, and Christian conversion is understood to happen as non-Christians join and gradually accept the message of Jesus. They, in turn, invite their friends to join them in forming another group. In this way the church self-perpetuates, forming a new cell group with each cycle. Such small groups help bring about the contextualisation of the church as it becomes focused around different cultural groups – young people, single parents, the over-sixties, people from a specific ethnic group, or those from a working-class or middle-class background. Nevertheless, it is important that such groups relate to one another and to the 'mother' church, to foster a rich diversity of membership.

The church of the new millennium will be the church of many small groups. Some of these may meet on church premises and be drawn from different ethnic or socio-economic backgrounds. Others may meet in a tightly zoned geographic area, where two or three couples of the same socio-economic background meet together and form their own neighbourhood cell. Some groups may share a specific interest, background, workplace or experience; others may consist of ex-offenders, unemployed young people, executives, housewives, divorced or singles, artists or young people.

In Share Jesus we ask many of our local church leaders to identify at least ten people-groups in their area and to make initial contact with them. Churches which do this, and which use mission teams to help them, have the most effective mission experiences. I recently came across a list of people-groups which one of our host churches identified on a rough estate in Glasgow. They found that there were single parents, bingo fans, workingmen's club regulars, street kids, elderly shut-ins, alcoholics anonymous and drug users. Their strategy for mission was based not around 'reaching the area', but around getting alongside these groups, winning their confidence, meeting their needs and witnessing in real-life situations.

From the information gleaned in the community survey, then, it should be possible to identify groups of people in your community who are unreached and in need of a Saviour. This is important information in devising a strategy for a local church to grow.

6. Developing aims and goals

Using the techniques outlined above, it should be possible to arrive at a number of priorities for evangelism in your area. As the church leadership team meet together, they should begin to identify realistic and achievable goals for their local mission. These should be prioritised and ways identified in which they might be accomplished.

It is vital that there is joint ownership of these goals by the whole congregation. Achieving them will be costly in terms of energy, finance and commitment, and it is crucial that there is broad agreement on what the priorities are. There should probably only be about two or three in total and, most important, they should be achievable! Some examples of aims and goals identified by churches working with us at Share Jesus include:

Deepening the spiritual life
To renew the devotional life of the church corporately and individually; to draw the membership together into closer fellowship; to seek fresh vision and hope for the future.

Proclaiming the faith within the local community
To highlight the profile of the church within the community; to break down the cultural gap between church and society; to make practical links of friendship with the community; to seek to bring them into a living relationship with Jesus Christ.

Outreach among teenagers
To encourage the development of youth work within the church, if necessary beginning new groups; to make contact with teenagers outside the church; to seek to lead them to Christ; to begin some kind of initial contact with detached young people in the community.

Mission among children
To engage in mission among children, seeking to strengthen existing children's work; to tell 'the Jesus story' in imaginative and exciting ways to children in the neighbourhood.

There are as many different aims and goals as there are churches. Others examples are identified in Appendix 3.

7. Writing a vision statement

If you were involved in the management of a business or corporation, you would be foolish indeed if you did not engage in strategic management:

> Forecasting is any attempt, usually based on past performance,
> to predict future outcomes and trends in the future
> environment of an organisation. *(G A Cole)*

The world is changing, society is changing, people are changing. If anything, this rate of change is accelerating! Any business wanting to survive must be aware of this and constantly adjust itself. Good businesses do not react to change after it has happened – they are actively predicting change and responding to it even before it occurs. If a church is to be effective in evangelism, it needs to be regularly reviewing its life in the light of the changing mission-context in which it is set.

When I took part in a management conference for entrepreneurial business people in Sheffield, I discovered that most fast-growing companies have a 'vision statement' – a declaration of where the organisation is headed in the next five or ten years. It has been encouraging to see that many churches around the UK have been adopting mission statements in recent years as they seek to define what they are trying to do and how they are trying to do it. Very few churches, however, have yet identified the importance of a vision statement (see Appendix 4). This sets the future course, charts the way ahead, and sets goals for development and growth for the coming years. It is little wonder, then, that many churches have no real strategy for growth, expansion and development. They are too busy with 'now' to think about 'tomorrow'. But churches which don't anticipate growth or plan for new life are unlikely to achieve them.

Anyone who has taken a course in contemporary management will know of the popular writings of Charles Handy, the well-known executive's guru. His concept of the 'Sigmoid Curve' is very relevant to many churches today. Handy suggests that every organisation, institution, group or team comes to a point where it 'peaks' in its effectiveness and performance. Only by constant self-assessment and appraisal can the organisation identify the 'flattening out' of its performance, and when this happens it must develop a new initiative, a new challenge, a new entrepreneurial vision, a new means of serving the market, and build towards another peak. If it fails to do this, it will surely decline.

As a church tries to formulate its vision, the congregation must be consulted so that they take ownership of the aims and goals identified. If local people understand the importance of these aims and goals, they are more likely to get involved and to feel included as the mission strategy develops. Every goal should be thought of as a 'faith target' and as such should be affirmed and celebrated. As these aims and goals are drawn together into a statement that the whole church owns, the shared vision should shape the direction of the church's mission and all of its ongoing plans and objectives. I believe that the whole process will encourage church members to look at the bigger picture and see beyond the immediacy of their need for a new boiler or a better signboard! It can develop a sense of hope, which is a gift of the Holy Spirit. It is this visionary hope which looks to Jesus as the Lord of the harvest, and which recognises that his commission to 'go into all the world' is just as relevant to churches as to individuals. This is not the end but the beginning. It is the start of a new determination by the congregation to move out from behind the walls of their church life and into effective mission in the world.

Book references: Donald McGavran, quoted in 'A Church Growth Look at Here's Life America', *Church Growth: America*, January-February 1977; Peter Anthony, *Managing Culture*, Open University Press, 1994; G A Cole, *Strategic Management*, D P Publications, 1994.

Chapter 7

PLANNING A LOCAL CHURCH-BASED MISSION

In 1984 I took about sixty people on a mission based in churches around north London. We called the project 'Share Jesus' to remind us that, whatever else we did, our most important task was to introduce Jesus to others. Since then Share Jesus has grown dramatically. Every year around five hundred Christians in the UK join me on this week-long mission, and about the same number engage in similar events across the United States of America. A new branch of Share Jesus has just started in Australia, and several other national churches are planning their own projects.

Back in 1984 I discovered that the best evangelists are not necessarily ministers or church leaders, but ordinary Christian men and women. To be effective in evangelism, you don't need a degree in theology or a three-year course on mission. When ordinary people launch out into mission, God anoints them and uses them in a special way. I believe this is because he sees his people becoming dependent upon him. They have recognised that they can't do this work in their own strength, and they want to work in partnership with him.

Christians who have never been on mission, or who belong to a church which is not mission-minded, are missing out! When ordinary Christians move out to witness in the parks, the pubs, the schools and the streets, they move out of their comfort zone. The work of mission brings us to a place of personal inadequacy and weakness, where we have to rely on God's guidance for the right words to say and the right things to do. This place of vulnerability is the best place for Christians to be.

All four Gospels end with Jesus Christ instructing his disciples to evangelise. The best known reference is in Matthew, often called 'the great commission':

> 'All authority in heaven and on earth has been given to me. Therefore go and make disciples of all nations, baptising them in the name of the Father and of the Son and of the Holy Spirit, and teaching them to obey everything I have commanded you. And surely I am with you always, to the very end of the age.'

The Christian faith is a faith to give away. The scriptures are constantly encouraging us to share our faith in Christ with others. The most important motivation for evangelism is the love of God. The gospel is not to be shared in a pushy way, but in a style that demonstrates God's love.

What is a mission?

When I first began to talk about mission to ministers in 1984, I didn't find much enthusiasm. Their mental image was usually of an evangelist, a week-long programme of evening 'rallies', bus-loads of other Christians coming in to hear the 'big name preacher', a huge choir, and all the trappings of what people call a 'crusade'. Many were very antagonistic to this format for mission, saying that they had 'tried it but it didn't work', that it was 'blatant emotional manipulation' or just plain old-fashioned. The general view was that such endeavours produced little lasting fruit and were followed by a huge feeling of anti-climax in the local church. I had to make it clear again and again that what they thought of as 'mission' and what I was proposing were two very different things! Even so, some couldn't be persuaded to give our 'Share Jesus' style of evangelism a try.

I have been fighting this kind of prejudice ever since. Much of my work over fifteen years as National Evangelist for the Methodist Church has been about persuading church leaders to take a fresh look at the potential of local, church-based missions. It has often been an up-hill task trying to introduce them to new models of evangelism which are about empowering Christians to share Jesus in their neighbourhoods, and to persuade them that traditional models which aim to 'bring the community to the church' are dead. In a highly secularised society, church-based missions must be about bridging the gap between the church and the community, about building real relationships with local people, and about Christians sharing their faith with people where they are. It is about taking the church out into the world.

I have seen that a period of mission in a church can be one of the most renewing, stimulating and fruitful phases in its life. I believe that churches should undertake missions at least every two or three years and that these should be part of realising the church's vision statement (see the previous chapter). Mission is a special time for Christians to move beyond the church walls and to take the gospel into the community. It enables them to meet non-Christians in a non-threatening way. Mission activities are a way of starting a conversation about Jesus and an opportunity to share his love.

The leaders, church council and congregation should really want a mission and need to pledge their support to make the week's work worthwhile. If only a small number of the congregation are keen, it will result in a very poor mission. Using the techniques outlined in the previous chapter, it should be possible to arrive at a vision statement and to agree a number of priorities for evangelism in the local area. The church leadership should discuss these goals, prioritise them and identify ways in which they might be accomplished. Faith-sharing should always be the central activity of the programme, and at every stage of planning everyone should stop to ask, 'How is this helping us to fulfil Jesus' great commission?'

Over the following pages I have outlined some concepts for a church-based mission. This is not a blueprint, but an example of how a church (perhaps supported by a visiting team) can engage in evangelism in their community.

Getting started

Naturally, churches can undertake a period of mission on their own, but my experience suggests that the project is much more effective if the church hosts an 'away team'. The whole thing takes on a powerful new dynamic when Christians from other churches come and help during the mission week. When the same gospel is spoken by fresh voices, it seems to cut more ice! An incoming team generates extra excitement and commitment locally, and such missions become a two-way activity, with the churches hosting the event renewed and the visiting team members transformed by the experience.

It is important that the incoming team's leader visits the church well in advance, possibly about six months before the mission. The afternoon can begin with a meal and an honest time of sharing with the minister. It is crucial that there is a high degree of trust between the visitor and the minister. The visiting leader must pledge to support the minister both publicly and privately at all stages of the mission process, or untold damage in the church could result.

During the evening of this pre-visit, the visitor can also meet with the church council to discuss the local situation, to view the aims and goals of the church, and to participate with other leaders in constructing a programme for the week of mission. The primary aim of the programme should be to empower everyone to share the good news about Jesus in the wider community. The secondary aim is to begin some of the 'new work' identified in the vision statement. This new work will need to be owned and fully supported by the congregation for at least twelve months after the mission has finished.

Mission programmes don't just happen: they come together after a great deal of planning and hard work. As the church leaders begin to prepare for the mission, they will constantly need to ask, 'Who? What? Where? When? How?' Deadlines must be set and individuals given specific areas of responsibility. Members of the congregation should be encouraged to own the mission from the earliest stages. A

95

local 'facilities' committee could prepare for the visiting team's arrival, welfare, food and transport, while another group might take responsibility for the planning of the mission programme.

The more that people on the fringes of church life are involved in organising and implementing the programme, the more fruitful the mission will be. We always encourage the church to draw in people from outside to help with preparation and to facilitate things like barbecues, sports days and barn dances. The more these people have a share in what's going on, the more likely it is that they will attend and come under the message of the gospel.

Hosting a team

Any church hosting a team must accept that the team is not coming to 'do the work' but to share as partners in mission. They must be willing to invest in the lives of each team member as well as to receive what each has to offer. Our experience has shown that missions are most effective when one team is commissioned to work with one congregation, no matter how small that congregation may be. This 'away team' can encourage 'growth thinking' in the church and act as a catalyst for change. This doesn't happen if one team tries to service several churches at once.

The team's witness is most powerful when its members come from a wide range of backgrounds, educational experience and churchmanship. All they need to share in common is a love for Jesus and a desire to share the faith in contemporary ways. At Share Jesus, most of our teams have a mix of age groups, though some teams may be predominantly made up of one age group. We recognise that both younger and older people on the teams are 'today's' church, so we value their individual gifts and encourage them to grow in the Christian life.

When the team arrives, the local people should host an event to welcome them. This first meeting will provide an opportunity to commission everyone, including the home team, for witness during the mission. The programme should provide lots of opportunities for the away team to pray and work with the home team so that there is no possibility of an 'us and them' culture developing. The aim is for everyone to be enriched by the partnership.

I am committed to this method of local church-based evangelism. After experiencing these missions in hundreds of different situations over the years, in a project which has involved thousands of different team members, I can only say, 'It works!' Every church could host a mission and, if they did, I'm sure they would experience growth. The results are three-fold. The combined witness of the local church and the visiting team is very effective, and lots of outsiders find a real faith in Jesus. Through the mission, the local church gains confidence to move beyond its doors and make a diverse range of new contacts. Finally, the visiting team is changed forever; God may lead many of them into Christian ministry as a result of their mission experience.

Looking back across fifteen years of mission, the three most popular objectives identified by churches have been:

- To raise the church's profile in the local community.
- To begin new work with teenagers.
- To develop the work with children.

These aims must be seen as part of a church's ongoing mission to its community. Taking these three aims as an example, I will now highlight ways in which they could be given special emphasis during a week of local mission.

1. Connecting with the community

Our Christian witness in the community should always be accompanied by expressions of genuine service, and a special time of mission is no exception. We must not only speak of the love of Jesus but demonstrate it in practical ways. Mission teams that visit the housebound, give a few hours of respite for carers or offer support for young parents, will impact those who wouldn't be reached through an open-air meeting or gospel concert. In a tightly knit community, many people will get to hear that the team's faith is not just about worship on Sunday but about practical service throughout the week. A mission team which operates as an 'evangelistic unit' without a genuine spirit of service and compassion will lack credibility. In fact everything that a team does should have the hallmark of Christlike compassion and love.

The door-to-door plan

Some techniques of door-to-door evangelism are a major turn-off. As I was writing this section, my doorbell rang and I was harassed for over twenty minutes by two earnest Jehovah's Witnesses. It was a text-book example of how to alienate and irritate someone. They were full of proof-texts and they wanted to discuss one obscure Bible passage after another. There was a hardness about their presentation which irritated me and a frustrating unwillingness to hear what I was saying. They didn't leave me with any desire to meet them again or go to their church. They hadn't taken time to cultivate a relationship and they didn't seem to care about me as a human being. They were simply reciting their 'patter'.

However, I'm sure that it is still crucially important to visit people in their homes. One of the most effective ways of doing this is for the host church to find a way of visiting a selected band of housing regularly. Effective door-to-door witness should be an ongoing activity. It is far better to visit a hundred houses four times a year than a thousand houses once every five years! The goal of the church shouldn't be to drop thousands of leaflets through letterboxes, but rather to develop a dozen good relationships. A mission-minded church could engage in door-to-door witness by taking round special invitations or magazines several times a year. This could be repeated year by year until real relationships develop and the visits become part of local life. When this kind of groundwork has been laid, door-to-door work in the context of a mission is much more effective. The church member who has been visiting a certain street for a year or more can take one of the visiting team along to introduce them to the contacts they have already made on their round. This process brings a far greater possibility of success in inviting them to special outreach events than if a 'cold contact' call was made.

The street dynamic

Some forms of Christian open-air witness are so embarrassingly bad, they have made me feel ashamed to be a Christian! But it doesn't have to be this way. I was in Leicester Square in London a few months ago when I came across four young men who were singing 'barbershop' in a superb and professional way. A crowd of around two hundred people gathered, and as their show continued they featured 'spirituals' like 'Gonna lay down my sword and shield' and 'Dry Bones'. The quality of their performance was as good as anything in the theatres across the street on Shaftesbury Avenue. Gradually they introduced short testimonies between the songs, and the performance became a powerful and positive witness. During local church missions we have used escapologists, street-theatre performers, choirs, fire-eaters, unicyclists and even trapeze artists to draw a crowd and introduce passers-by to the good news about Jesus.

The street dynamic is about getting into the places where people are and becoming a part of their everyday lives. Good street theatre and music can raise a church's profile in an area, publicise other events and become a contact point for meeting people and witnessing to them.

Community celebrations

Over recent years, our teams have developed programmes called 'random acts of kindness' in which they do things for the local community with no other motive than to be kind. I once saw a team give out 500 ice-cold cans of Coke in a town centre one sweltering day in California, and I am sure it got people talking about the mission much more than would a glossy colour brochure.

I believe every church should try to organise regular community evangelistic events every year. When I was a minister, we used to organise an outreach bonfire party on 5th November. We distributed tickets around the whole community and besides a professional firework display, a massive bonfire and good music, there was an eight-minute 'epilogue' while people munched their baked potatoes. To the hundred people standing in our church hall, it was a brief opportunity to reflect about life and faith. More importantly, it became a focus for our church's programme of evangelism and an opportunity for the congregation to introduce their friends to the church community.

This kind of event can be the highlight of the mission. Where there is already a history of community events, it will be particularly effective. During the church missions Share Jesus co-ordinate, we sometimes organise community activities such as a barn dance with a Christian caller, a summer barbecue with a guest singer, or a community sports day with a picnic tea and a visiting Christian sports personality. The presentation of the faith at these events only lasts for a few minutes and is usually integral to the programme of the day. Some of the missions we co-ordinate are like community festivals, and their witness may be based round a carnival procession, a series of sophisticated arts events, a 'country fayre' with sideshows, or a sequence of biblical floral displays. I've seen teams constructing a replica of Noah's Ark on the back of a lorry, co-ordinating a Christian opera performance, organising a bookstall at a country fair, and putting together a flower show in a church sanctuary in a busy tourist centre. These are important opportunities for raising the church's profile, connecting with the local community and sharing literature about Jesus. When the church reconnects with the community in this way, we are able to speak to people where they are and gain a hearing which wouldn't be possible 'within the chapel walls'.

2. Connecting with kids

Church-based children's work has become a Cinderella ministry in the life of the church. It is under-resourced and often
unimaginative and ineffective. Yet many committed
Christians took their first steps of faith when they were children.

Children are the emerging generation and we need to
determine ways of reaching them which are contemporary
and relevant. Very often our children's work uses techniques
that were effective forty years ago but which have long-since
passed their sell-by date. If we want to know where 5–10
year-olds are at today, we need to watch Saturday morning
television. It's a very hi-tech, glitzy, multi-media, pop-orien-
tated approach, with items lasting for no more than three or
four minutes. Mission among children will increasingly
demand that we use hi-tech audio-visual resources and create
imaginative programmes. Paper and crayons are no longer
sufficient to attract their attention or speak to them about
Jesus.

It is important to understand something of child development, too. Children under six, for example, have random
patterns of thinking and an inability to distinguish reality
from fantasy. There's often a confusion between miracles
and magic. One of the most important things we can do for
children of this age is to show a loving acceptance of them,
even when they are disruptive. A child's world usually cen-
tres on their mum and/or dad, and we must learn how to
relate to that world. Children under six generally 'experience' faith. Through their experiences of security, respon-
siveness and openness they discover that God can be trusted;
through being valued as an individual they find God's love;
through the repair of friendships they discover repentance
and reconciliation. The more we develop these important
and positive experiences, the more we communicate the love
of Christ.

The characteristics of 7–10 year-olds are very different.
They have begun to think sequentially, are often hungry for

knowledge and able to think in concrete terms. They have great loyalties to teams or groups and can generally distinguish reality from fantasy. The activities we devise must be stimulating, exciting and usually participatory. There is often the development of an 'affiliation faith' at this age in which children discover commitment to Jesus by belonging to Christian groups.

Children aged over eleven have often discovered that their image is important. They identify closely with small groups of friends, and are often beginning to ask big questions about meaning and purpose. They want to discover who they are. Abstract thinking and the questioning of authority are other hallmarks of this age group. This is the time for 'searching faith' when questions need to be discussed and answers sought. We mustn't underestimate the seriousness of their quest for meaning.

In the ongoing mission of a local church we need to think creatively and radically. Does the Sunday school have to meet on a Sunday? How can mission programmes not only identify new groups of kids, but also facilitate their nurture in exciting and relevant ways? One of the most effective 'Sunday schools' in the country meets at my local church every Thursday evening. The eighty children taking part pay towards the cost of one video rental. There's a waiting list to join. Skilled drama teachers explore the Bible stories using role-play, drama games and kids' performances. The parents queue at the door to watch! One of the best ways to reach adults is through their children, but we only gain a hearing from children if we invest high levels of energy and imagination in the programme.

A special week of mission provides a great opportunity for highlighting this kind of project, and many of our mission teams co-ordinate high-energy kids' clubs as part of their programme. It's all the more effective if this kind of work is already an ongoing part of church life. One word of important advice, however. It is crucial that the legal safeguards regarding adults working with children are properly adhered to. Every worker should have references and sign a written declaration regarding the Children Act before we can let them care for children. And every church should formulate a policy for child protection. Advice on doing this can be obtained from the Methodist Education and Youth, Methodist Church House, 25 Marylebone Road, London, NW1 5JR.

Some of the kids' mission activities we use at Share Jesus include the following:

Family devotions
This involves visiting families joining local families for team-devotions each morning. The emphasis is on participation, with children of all ages taking part in music, drama, readings and quizzes.

Kids holiday clubs
These normally function each morning of a mission (during school holidays) from just after 10 in the morning to just before 12 noon. (To comply with legal safeguards, we would recommend that clubs last less than two hours.) The emphasis is on fun, games, activities and creativity, often following the kind of programmes devised by agencies like Scripture Union.

Backyard clubs
Groups of local kids invite their friends to an afternoon club in their own backyard. Games and a barbecue are followed by a short Bible-story sequence.

Evening activities
Camp-fires, sports nights, treasure hunts and team games are all good ways of getting kids involved. Friendships established between leaders and children will lead many to faith in Jesus.

3. Connecting with youth

The youth scene is constantly changing and what was 'in' last week is surely 'out' this! The techniques which worked with teens last year probably won't work this year. Many of us have to face up to the fact that the era of the youth club, with table-tennis tables and dartboards, is largely over. The groups which seem to be most effective are largely activity-based, where young people constantly shape their own programme.

However, mission among young teenagers can be very rewarding. Some of the neediest young people in our communities today are detached from any kind of regular youthwork. Some of them are missing out on regular schooling, while others have become strangers to a normal life at home. Yet these are some of the kids who are most open to the good news about Jesus. But to reach them is a costly business.

There are a number of stages of adolescence which we should be aware of in our planning. The 11–14 year-old phase is often known as the 'same sex' stage in which young people identify closely with small gangs of their peers. Then there is the transitional stage from 15–16 years, a time of very few close friends, crushes and moodiness. This is followed by the 'sexual discovery' stage and the search for a steady relationship.

One of the hallmarks of adolescence is a great feeling of insecurity, often connected with poor feelings of self-image and 'how I look'. It's an era of marked intellectual growth and of great pressure at school. There are major emotional developments, often accompanied by highs and lows, and there are the social developments connected with working through personal insecurities. Teenagers begin to identify with ideas and to own ways of thinking. It is often the time for personal commitment to Jesus Christ and to a life lived totally for him. Some of the youth activities we have found effective in recent years have included the following:

Teens club
This gives the team and the young people a chance to get to know each other. Offer a full programme of activities for younger teenagers, such as barbecues and night hikes, or sleepovers in the church hall (with lots of leaders present!).

Pioneer outreach
This is work among detached young people in the neighbourhood. Perhaps a gang of teenagers gathers in the local park each evening and, at present, there is no contact with the church. Hanging around with them and bringing them back to the church for coffee and burgers could be the start of ongoing contact and witness.

Nurture group
This involves a team-led study course for young people already in the orbit of church life. Leisure and fun activities mixed with interactive Bible study and fellowship are led by other teens on the team. They work on bringing young people to faith and releasing them into ministry.

Youth events
Resources such as Christian rock bands, drama groups, dance companies and DJs are given space to communicate the faith in contemporary ways. Young people are given the opportunity to make a personal response to Jesus Christ.

Creating a mission programme

The mission programme should encourage creativity and fun, and be a genuine expression of the love of Christ. The possibilities for the week are limitless. I am constantly amazed at the way in which local churches evolve imaginative programmes for sharing the faith. The golden rule is that mission should never, ever be boring, and usually it should be inexpensive. The more mission events involve local people in preparation and participation, the more likely it is that they will be well-supported. Here is a list of suggestions for other types of activity:

School assemblies and classroom presentations
Multi-cultural events (often involving food!)
Glorious garden parties, with lots of time for chatting
Christian apologetics evenings (eg science and faith)
Community conferences talking about the future

Music celebrations and concerts
Flower festivals, maybe using a biblical theme
Games evenings with team interviews
Pilgrimages to historic Christian sites
Sponsored events with visitors and locals participating
Pub meetings with seminars or discussions
'Colour me beautiful' programmes
Sports coaching sessions
Lectures on subjects such as stress, parenting or bereavement
Barbecues, picnics and banquets
Evangelistic preaching

To demonstrate how a mission might be structured, see the sample programme in Appendix 5. It shows how one team can be used in two ways – with half the team made up of teenagers and students (Group A) and the other consisting of older Christians (Group B). The programme is based round a seven-day mission trying to achieve the goals outlined above. Evidently different goals would demand a different programme, but the overriding question at every stage of planning should always be 'How can we effectively witness for Christ in every aspect of this programme?'

PART 3
The Heart of Evangelism

Chapter 8

A STRATEGY FOR EVANGELISM

Without doubt, prosperous urbanised countries such as the United Kingdom are the most difficult to evangelise. In such societies, we are faced with a decline in understanding about Christianity and a new generation that seems particularly hardened to the claims of Jesus Christ. Our impact on society's belief systems is diminishing at a greater rate than our ability to make new church members. In just twenty-five years there has been a remarkable change in the popular perception of Jesus. A Gallup survey of 1957 found that 71% of those who responded believed Jesus to be the Son of God, while 9% looked on him as 'just a man'. By 1982, however, a detailed research project undertaken by Leeds University revealed that only 43% saw him as the Son of God, while 30% saw him as 'an ordinary human being'. People have been turning away from a popular faith in Jesus by the million. But why?

Many people have a perspective on life that is shaped by the secular culture in which they live. If we want to be effective in this mission field, we must become familiar with the voices that are driving society today.

- The pluralist says, 'What's true for me is true, and what's true for you is true.' But Christianity teaches there is only one eternal truth, and only one true way. Ultimate truth is to be found in Jesus Christ.

- The modernist says, 'We're all cogs in a machine; we're all disposable. Nothing matters.' But the Christian argues

that we are all precious to God, unique, loved and
known by the One who gives us life.

- The relativist says, 'There are no rights and wrongs – it
  all depends on circumstances.' But our faith teaches us
  that there *is* right and wrong, good and evil – and we
  have the free will to choose the right way.

- The secularist says, 'Religion is a thing of the past. It has
  no relevance to life today.' But the Christian recognises
  that, whatever happens, God's kingdom will continue to
  grow and nothing in this world or the next can defeat it.

- The hedonist says, 'Eat, drink and be merry, for tomorrow we die.' But the Christian must remind him, 'After
  this comes judgement.'

- The futurist says, 'We're powerless to change anything.
  It's all pointless anyway.' But the Christian perspective is
  based on the almighty power of God and the belief that
  prayer changes things.

Ultimately, the gospel looks at life in a totally different way
to other world views. However, if we don't have some understanding of these perspectives, we will not be equipped to
confront them. When witnessing to people, we are likely to
face difficult questions and challenges to our faith.
Evangelism is essentially a spiritual task: this is why we need
others to pray for us so that we will be protected and
empowered for the task.

Often the church seems to have lost its way in its evangelism. I believe there are five key areas where the church should
direct its energy and resources in the highly secularised society of the West. These five areas should form the church's
evangelistic agenda for mission in the third millennium.

I. Unreached people-groups

Britain today is a mission field. With only around 2% of the
population in regular attendance at Christian worship, and

steeply declining church membership statistics in the major church denominations, we have an awesome task before us!

According to research done by MARC Europe, there are people-groups around the United Kingdom who are completely unreached by the Christian gospel. Around 1,500 people living in small private developments on the edge of Rossendale, for example, are employed in management, commerce and blue collar industrial work. Their main need is for local friendship and support, and the challenge is to question their materialistic lifestyle. Among them there are no known Christians and no known evangelistic outreach.

Over 20,000 Asians have come from India and Bangladesh to live and work around Blackburn. There is large-scale unemployment. Many cannot read and write English, their mother tongue being either Gujarati or Urdu, their religion Islam. There is no known Christian witness among them.

About 300 gypsies and travellers live on a permanent site near Norwich. There are a large number of children and teenagers among them. Many of them feel marginalised or rejected by society. Although some have a Roman Catholic background, there are no known Christians among them.

In towns and cities all over the country, increasing numbers of people fall outside the influence and witness of the church. The continuing decline in the use of religious buildings for 'rites of passage' such as the naming of children, weddings and funerals means that fewer and fewer people come into contact with the living community of believers. The urgent evangelistic task is for Christians to relocate to these areas and to witness among these unreached people through practical service and effective dialogue. Too many churches are so preoccupied with the people on the fringes of their church life, they have no time to reach out to those who are completely beyond the fringe.

2. The task of apologetics

I write this following a stressful week spent talking to

teenagers. First came the recording of a short television series for ITV called *Youth Dilemmas* in which I discussed parents, sex and clubbing with a group of teenagers who included my son! It wasn't easy trying to put forward my views on these subjects as a parent and a Christian to a peer group that seems largely to have dismissed the moral and ethical boundaries I grew up with. Later in the week I was the guest at a north London senior school. In the morning I faced about 150 sixteen-year-olds, and roughly the same number of fifteen-year-olds, in the afternoon at a conference about science and faith. Handling their questions certainly wasn't easy!

A government survey of the religious attitudes of secondary school pupils illustrates that the task of evangelism among teens is getting harder. Over a twelve-year period, the number of teenagers who could say, 'God is real to me' had almost halved from 41% to 22%. Over the same period those finding it hard to believe in God rose dramatically from 36% to 50%. We urgently need to discover ways to demonstrate that Christianity is credible to this generation.

Another detailed research project, conducted by the Rev Dr Henry Gibson in 1989 among 6,838 secondary school pupils aged between 11 and 17 years in the Dundee area, came up with some fascinating statistics. His research indicated that for many teenagers science alone can explain 'spiritual' phenomena and science is the only key to all truth. Scientistic attitudes such as these appear to increase with age among the sample. Around 30% of the group believed that human beings are just complex chemical machines. Dr Gibson concluded: 'There is consistent drift from the churches and from the Christian faith ... Attitudes to science do appear to influence attitudes to Christianity and vice versa.'

I am convinced that a major task of evangelism is to address people's conflict between science and Christian faith. Several years ago I undertook a fascinating tour called 'The Truth About Science' which was sponsored by the Evangelical Alliance. Astrophysicist and university chaplain,

Dr David Wilkinson, and I visited some twenty towns and spoke to over 10,000 people. Each night we were accompanied by an internationally renowned scientist who was a committed Christian. It was a piece of mission work quite unlike anything I'd previously done. The people who came to the presentation tended to be quite intellectual, and many of them were not committed Christians. During the course of the evening, our presentation explored the relationship between science and faith, and argued that the Christian message is credible intellectually. We went on to explore the deep philosophical questions about origin and purpose which science throws up but which it cannot answer. The response was overwhelming. Hundreds of people from the audience took home literature about the Christian faith, and many stayed behind for prayer there and then.

As our society grows more secularised and the reservoir of Christian understanding evaporates, the evangelist will increasingly have to provide an apologetic for the Christian faith. We can no longer assume that people know the Christian story, let alone understand it. Increasingly, we will have to take our place in the marketplace of religious ideas and philosophical theories and make a credible 'defence' of this faith which means so much to us.

3. Dialogue with people of other faiths

The growth of popular understanding about science, philosophy, comparative religion and psychotherapy has brought many other explanations of meaning into the public arena. The rise of non-Christian religion in the United Kingdom rose from 538,321 adherents in 1970 to a projected 2,430,000 by the year 2000 (*Christian England*, 1991). Between 1970 and 2000 it is thought that the number of practising Buddhists in the UK will have grown from 6,000 to 40,000; Hindus from 50,000 to 220,000; Sikhs from 1,500 to 20,000; and Muslims from 250,000 to 1,500,000.

The presence of non-Christian religious groups poses a great challenge for Christian mission. Some Christians are so committed to welcoming and affirming these other faith communities, they practically suspend the call to share Jesus Christ with them.

Dialogue is a fundamental part of any mission, and its hallmarks must be genuine openness and interaction. Through talking to adherents of other faiths we can learn about their customs, religious awareness, values and assumptions about life. This dialogue is an integral part of the basic missionary task and, accompanied by the development of long-term relationships, is the only way to win people of other faiths to Christ. In any such contact with people, it is imperative that we avoid unnecessary controversy and resist the temptation to quarrel or criticise. It is better to lose an argument than to lose a relationship. We are most likely to win someone for Christ through loving them rather than defeating them! However, we must take every opportunity to say what we believe and why we believe it. Personal testimony in such situations is important.

We also need to ask God to give us a deep love and compassion for people of other faiths. Indeed, it may be appropriate for us to say sorry for the ways in which our imperialist culture has adversely affected their lives and the lives of their forebears. Over recent years hundreds of Christians have been following the old routes of the Crusades, apologising to the Muslim people for the many injustices and cruel deeds done all those years ago in the name of Christ. They have encountered a warm and emotional response and sensed a new openness to begin again.

The Asian community is very hospitable. It is almost impossible to drop into an Asian home for just a few minutes. Hospitality is of enormous importance in the East, and people are often thrilled when others visit them at home. Many Asians in the UK have little experience or understanding of the British as a people of prayer and devotion. Indeed, many of them see the church as corrupt and Western culture as decadent. We have a lot of groundwork to do before any real sharing can begin.

One of our mission teams was working with an Asian Christian fellowship. They started up a series of 'English as a second language' house groups for women who were struggling with English speech and culture. The love, sharing and openness which the team found at these groups was remarkable, and many deep conversations about Jesus took place in them. It was just this kind of multi-cultural situation in which the gospel first took hold and in which those who were hostile to Christianity were converted. The apostle Paul is a good example:

> I was personally unknown to the churches of Judea that are in Christ. They only heard the report: 'The man who formerly persecuted us is now preaching the faith he once tried to destroy.' And they praised God because of me.

I have met a number of people from other religious backgrounds in the UK who have accepted Christ as Saviour; they include Hindus, Buddhists, Jews and Muslims. Effective witness among people of other faiths can be done, as long as it is done in the right way and with the right sensitivity. I'm hoping for more of this in the coming years.

4. Witness to New Agers

The growth of phenomena such as New Age thinking, star signs, meditation and alternative medicine has brought a plethora of new religious perspectives. In North America more than 1,200 newspapers carry astrology columns. A Gallup survey among British teenagers in the mid-1980s revealed that over 50% of them said they believed that astrology worked in some form.

This plurality of meaning is the driving force behind secularism and runs contrary to Christian mission. Once the church cornered the market on meaning, but now Christianity is seen as just one among many options. The church has largely failed to understand this tide of new religious interpretations. Browse any high-street bookstore and you will quickly discover that the religious section is dominated by New Age philosophy and spirituality. A vast network of New Age retail outlets is springing up all over the country.

The definitive belief of New Agers is that we are moving out of the age of Pisces and into the age of Aquarius. The age of Christianity is now ending (the era of Pisces and the fish) and we are in transition to a new era. The spiritual energy flowing into the planet is focused along lines called 'ley-lines', and the places where these lines cross are called 'power points'. These energies are strongest when there is a full moon, and at the times of the equinoxes and solstices. They claim that the new age will be an age of service, of living in harmony, of attunement with the planet and with one another. It will be an age of groups and communities, of people living and working and learning together. It will be an age in which the whole is seen as greater than the sum of its parts (this concept is called synergy). The underlying thesis of the movement is that you don't need to obey a God distinct from yourself, because that idea is limiting; rather, you can do your own thing and connect with the divine power within yourself. In this way you will discover unlimited potential to transform yourself and the planet so that the new age of peace, light and love can begin. New Age influence is penetrating our society on every level – the media, psychology, education, politics, business and medicine. Evangelists working among New Agers tell us that when they give their Christian testimony, the response is 'How lovely'.

We need to be very careful in our definition of terms and in exploring what New Agers believe. For the New Ager, being 'spiritual' refers to getting in touch with one's divine self rather than submitting to the Trinity. 'Christ' refers to a level of consciousness we can all attain rather than a title only fitting for Jesus of Nazareth. 'Atonement' refers to the idea that we are already in union with God rather than being reconciled to him through Jesus Christ. The New Ager is loathe to discern any difference between their 'spiritual' experience and that of the committed Christian. If we point out the differences, they are likely to become angry and may even feel threatened. We must share Jesus with New Agers in a way that shows he is real to us, that is devoid of Christian jargon. The common starting-points for dialogue are our common value of creation and shared sense of responsibility for the created order. We need to point out that while our God suffuses his creation, he is also a person who is apart from it.

One of our Seed Teams, under the brave and pioneering leadership of a young lady from Belfast, has been building bridges with a large community of New Agers living on Cool Mountain outside Cork in Southern Ireland. After an initially hostile reception, the team have established a powerful Christian witness in the community. The witness has largely been through compassion, care and service. Slowly the residents have grown more confident with the Christians among them and have become more open to talking about faith and spirituality. Through love and care, the team have earned the right to talk about Jesus and to share the story of his work in their lives. A Christian prayer chapel has been established in the community and there is now a much more general acceptance of Christianity. What the Seed Team have modelled on Cool Mountain is something which everyone committed to evangelism among New Agers would do well to imitate.

5. Community-based evangelism

We have often seen evangelism as something 'cut off' from the rest of life. When Jesus talked about mission in the world, he talked about the tiny piece of leaven that makes the bread rise, the pinch of salt that brings flavour to everything it touches.

Of all the forms of evangelism most appropriate for the new millennium, I believe that community development is one of the most powerful and prophetic. It can also be one of the most effective. 'Community development' is a term used to describe a way not of providing things for people but of working with them so that they can help themselves. In this kind of mission Christians become involved in helping people to achieve their full potential. The concern is to develop the whole person: their spiritual, emotional, physical and social needs, and their sense of well-being. This is a long-term programme of evangelism which begins by meeting people in their needs, hopes and aspirations. When this happens the church becomes known as a place of belonging, of caring, of growth, for individuals. Eventually it becomes an integral part of the community.

Over the last few years, several of our Seed Teams missions have been based in urban priority areas, and have adopted the 'community development' model for mission as their guide. The results have been exciting. One team outside Glasgow developed a drop-in centre with a group of single mums in a tower-block. Rather than going 'door to door', the group evolved a centre known for caring, service and Christian witness. In another urban priority area, where the council was offering council houses for 50 pence (if you'd spend £25,000 to renovate them!), a retired couple moved in as a Seed Team to begin a programme of community development among people who felt disenfranchised and powerless. By working alongside their neighbours in many caring projects, they demonstrated the power and integrity of the Christian gospel.

On a 'priority need' estate, people don't normally go to church. As the church engages in community development, it helps the people with whom they are working to develop new ideas of what church is about. Gradually new relational networks are established and those who have had little or no contact with Christians begin to understand what Christians believe and why. In this way Christians can engage in the pressing issues of the estate and work alongside local people in tackling them. The signs of the kingdom are acted out in everyday life and Jesus Christ is celebrated not only in word but in deed. Experience has shown that the community soon begins to see that the gospel of Jesus really is good news for the poor, and is relevant to real life and real suffering. The community development style of mission can operate in suburbs, small towns, even in villages. I believe it to be one of the most effective ways of reaching a whole community with the gospel. Barry Osborne observed that churches who became most involved with the local community over the long term grew the most steadily:

> Those commenced by evangelistic mission usually started
> strongly but numbers dropped in following months or years,
> and sometimes the entire results of a mission dropped away.
> Those churches keen on contact with the rest of the
> community appeared to sustain steady growth.

Ultimately, the church should be like leaven in dough or salt in food. It will have a much greater long-term effect if it is immersed in the ongoing life of the community rather than by doing hit-and-run missions. Evangelism is about living Christ within the community. The slow but dynamic influence of a small group of people who really believe in Jesus can eventually transform a village, a town, a city, even a nation! The future is full of possibilities, and Christians are called to look beyond the needs of maintaining their denominational structures to the bigger vision of winning others for Christ. As we live the life he has called us to, both individually and corporately, we will begin to see people and places change. I believe he can use us to do things for him which are beyond our wildest imagining.

A vision for growth

Over the centuries, the Christian community has become an ever larger proportion of the world's population. In AD 1430 only 1% of the world's population was Christian; today it is 9%. The Christian church is, according to trustworthy figures, growing at three times the world's birth rate! If we measure by the growth of new believers, Christianity is the world's fastest growing global religion. Today, 600 million people out of 6 billion in the world are Bible-believing Christians.

Sadly, many Christians in the West have seemingly lost their confidence in the gospel. They are unwilling to die for their faith but would rather deny it. Many recognise that evangelism is a very costly and demanding activity and so choose to keep their faith to themselves.

> Then James and John, the sons of Zebedee, came to him.
> 'Teacher,' they said, 'we want you to do for us whatever we ask.'
>
> 'What do you want me to do for you?' he asked.
>
> They replied, 'Let one of us sit at your right and the other at your left in your glory.'
>
> 'You don't know what you are asking,' Jesus said. 'Can you drink the cup I drink or be baptised with the baptism I am baptised with?'
>
> 'We can,' they answered.
>
> Jesus said to them, 'You will drink the cup I drink and be baptised with the baptism I am baptised with...'

There are many pieces of equipment a contemporary evangelist may need for his task – a decent car, a good website, a mobile phone. But the most essential equipment for anyone with a vision for evangelism is the cup that Jesus offered, the cup of suffering. His whole life was committed to suffering in obedience to his Father's will, and to caring for those who suffer. Evangelism is far more credible when Christians are willing to enter into the sufferings of the world.

When I was preparing a radio programme for transmission a couple of days after the horrific shooting of so many innocent children in Dunblane, I called Victim Support in that town for an interview. After a couple of minutes the leader of this agency in Dunblane, a lady called Mary, asked, 'Is that wee Robbie?' I agreed that my name was Rob! She went on to tell me that she had re-committed her life to Christ at a meeting I'd led in Scotland. As part of her new commitment to Jesus she had got involved with Victim

Support, and now found herself at the centre of one of the nation's greatest tragedies.

The second essential piece of equipment for today's evangelist is the towel of service.

> Jesus called them together and said, 'You know that those who are regarded as rulers of the Gentiles lord it over them, and their high officials exercise authority over them. Not so with you. Instead, whoever wants to become great among you must be your servant, and whoever wants to be first must be slave of all. For even the Son of Man did not come to be served, but to serve, and to give his life as a ransom for many.'

During Easter People in 1999, I glimpsed through my hotel window the thousands of people walking expectantly down the street towards the massive Bournemouth International Centre. As I watched, I could hear the television news reporter describing the horrific pictures of the Kosovan refugees trekking wearily towards Albania. It seemed to me that what we were doing in our great evangelical celebrations was an anathema if we were somehow unresponsive to what was happening in the rest of the world. Later that evening I went onto the platform and told four thousand people how I felt. Between 9 am and 9 pm the following day Easter People collected over 14 tons of aid, purchased and insured a lorry, found two drivers and sent the precious cargo off to a church swamped with refugees in Southern Albania. They also collected £30,000 and despatched it within hours to relief agencies for specific projects among the refugees.

We have 'done evangelism' at Easter People for many years. Open-air meetings, posters, free tickets to musicals, distribution of tracts and street theatre. But nothing in all my experience had such an evangelistic impact on the town as this one act of kindness. As hundreds of people queued with blankets and pillows and cooking utensils, reporters from newspapers, TV and radio stations all over the region began to show up. Hundreds of townsfolk joined the queue, and the news of our effort spread like wildfire through hotels and shops as we became inundated with gifts for our relief effort. This one good deed did more to convince the townsfolk that our faith meant something real to us than any sophisticated media presentation. We can be big on words, but if we are short on deeds our message sounds hollow and empty.

The final piece of equipment for the evangelist to take with him for the task is the yoke of obedience. Essentially, evangelism is about obedience – total submission to Jesus Christ, willingness to go where he sends us and to speak on his authority. My vision for the evangelist of the new millennium is that each will carry with him the cup, the towel and the yoke – symbols of true servanthood and sacrifice.

What has always moved me about this story of James and John, and Jesus' challenge to them, is that history proved they were listening! We read in the book of Acts that King Herod had 'James, the brother of John, put to death with the sword'. James was the first of the twelve apostles to suffer martyrdom, and was killed during a time of Christian persecution under Herod Agrippa in AD 44. If we really would share Jesus in the new millennium, we follow in the footsteps of thousands of others who have gone before us, people like James who paid the ultimate price for their faithfulness to the message.

I know that God will continue to raise up new generations of Christians to stand firm in the gospel and take every opportunity to share Jesus in the ever growing work of building God's kingdom. The big question is, will you be a part of this strategy? Will you share in the greatest work we can ever do on earth – leading others to the Saviour, Jesus Christ?

Bible references: Galatians 1:22–24; Mark 10:35–44; Acts 12:2.

Book references: Barry Osborne, *A Second Workbook in Rural Evangelism*, Partners' Publication, Federation for Rural Evangelism, 1984.

Chapter 9

A BURDEN FOR EVANGELISM

The first proper mission I ever took part in was a harrowing experience. I was a student at Cliff College, a Bible college in Derbyshire's Peak District. We were sent to a rather spartan area near Sheffield, called Gleadless. I was dispatched by the team leader to go out onto the streets and find young people to come and see a film in the church hall. The streets were bare, and the drizzling rain swept across the urban sprawl. Eventually I came across a fish-and-chip shop with a crowd of leather-clad teenagers standing inside eating their chips. Rather nervously I invited them to see the film (which featured a rather young Cliff Richard, I seem to remember). To my amazement, they agreed to come.

I sauntered back to the church and about half an hour later the motorbikes roared up and they came inside. They sat on a table at the back of the room chewing gum and giggling, but no-one seemed to mind too much. At the end of the evening the evangelist made an appeal and, to my utter amazement, one of the bikers went forward and knelt at the front. He was led off to a counselling room where the gospel was shared and prayers were said. We said goodnight to him and his gang, and looked forward to welcoming them back the next day. That was not to be. Within two hours the young man was dead, killed in a tragic motorcycle accident.

I have never forgotten it. From this earliest experience of evangelism I came to recognise that Christian mission is not a game or something the church does to make up its numbers. It's a hallowed privilege, a commission none of us can honestly evade. Time and again across the years I have thought of that lad and my brief but important conversation with him on his last night on earth. It convinced me that evangelism is the church's most urgent task. In telling others we fulfil the very heart of the church's mission. The decisions made as a result are made for eternity. God forgive us if we don't tell others, for we miserably fail them and deny them the greatest opportunity of all – an opportunity to form a relationship with Jesus Christ, the Saviour of the world.

It is easy for the work of evangelism to become 'just another duty' or yet something more we've got to do. Whenever I lead teams on mission, I usually gather them together on the first evening for a private prayer session. I explain that without a God-given love for the place where we are on mission, and for the people among whom we are working, we will miss the true significance of what we are doing. In mission after mission and year after year, I've known the Lord give us that love. Sometimes it has been almost tangible – a heart-gripping kind of love which flows out in service, care and compassion. If we are to be effective in evangelism, we each need that kind of love, a love so profound that it expresses God's love for the world and humanity. As we enter into the enormity of this love, we share the privilege of becoming ambassadors for Christ.

Felt needs

It is easy for Christians to forget what it's like not to have a faith. We may have to cast our mind back many years to recall what life was like before we met Jesus. The comfort, strength, meaning and joy that our relationship with him has brought us have often become such an integral part of who we are, we take it for granted! In his letters to the first Christian churches, the apostle Paul often had to remind his readers what life used to be like before their conversion:

> Remember that at that time you were separate from Christ, excluded from citizenship in Israel and foreigners to the

covenants of the promise, without hope and without God in the world.

If we are to be effective in evangelism, we need to think our-selves into the feelings, lifestyle and circumstances of the people we are trying to reach.

Part of sensing a burden for others is to empathise with their circumstances and understand their situation. The gospel is most relevant where it matches another person's need. It also teaches that the person is unique and of incal-culable personal value:

> Each man, woman and child is of great value, not for some
> ulterior motive such as self gratification, or wealth or power or
> as a 'sex object' or for the 'good of society' – but because of his
> or her origin – God has created every human being in His own
> image. *(Francis Schaeffer)*

Only as I begin to understand the person I am witnessing to can I begin to apply my personal testimony to their unique situation.

What, then, are some of the greatest felt needs that people have in contemporary society today, and how can we begin to get a burden for them?

Security

John Naisbitt, an influential researcher of contemporary trends in American society, has written:

> As a society we are moving from the old to the new and we are
> still caught in motion. Caught between eras we experience
> turbulence, during turbulent times people need structure not
> ambiguity in their lives. This demand for structure will increase
> … people are looking for something to hang on to, not
> something to debate.

It's true. Millions of people are caught up in a whirl of mass redundancy and relocation, of regular divorce and marriage break-up (with the average couple only surviving nine years), of uncertain health and stressful situations in parenting. They are living in a society that's a roller-coaster of constant change and they are looking for something solid to hang on to.

The search for security has featured in the writings of many famous philosophers. James Boswell, in the eighteenth century, kept asking where the 'centre of a man' is. He was looking for the point of 'steadfastness' from which his needs could at last be known. Christians believe that the fixed point is Jesus – the Alpha and the Omega, the first and the last, the start and the finish, the one in whom everything finds its proper place. In a society looking for something to hang on to, we can point people to Jesus who is the source of all security and the rock-solid foundation on whom we can safely build our lives.

Meaning

We live in a materialistic society in which most of us are intent on acquiring more and more things. Some sociologists have noted that this consumerism isn't satisfying. Contemporary advertising persuades us not only to purchase things for their intrinsic usefulness, but as a means of reinforcing our personal identity. Unfortunately, in this process, the thing we strive to own can own us:

> I am not myself, I am what I have. My property constitutes myself and my identity. The thought in the statement 'I am I' is 'I am I because I have X, Y and Z' – i.e. all natural objects and persons to whom I relate myself through my power to control them, to make them permanently mine. In the having mode there is no alive relationship between me and what I have. It and I have become things, and I have it – because I have the force to make it mine. But there is also a reverse relationship – it has me, because my sense of identity rests upon my having it.
> *(Erich Fromm)*

The hedonistic pleasure-seeking materialism which envelops much of our society is leaving many people feeling empty and lost. They are looking for deeper meaning in their lives. Where they can't find it, feelings of futility and despair may come to dominate. The suicide rate among teenagers, for instance, rose by 33% between 1980 and 1990, and there were 100 reported attempts for every successful suicide. In one survey in Singapore in 1989, researchers discovered that 69% of teenagers went through some kind of experience of fairly serious depression during their adolescence. Telephone helplines continue to highlight the desperate needs experienced in our society today. In an average year, over 35,000 people call Alcoholics Anonymous, 50,000 phone for marriage guidance and around 400,000 call on the services of the Samaritans.

The things we own can never really add meaning to our lives. Only a living relationship with Jesus Christ can do that. He created us, he knows us and he sees the potential of what we could become. Our burden for those who feel that life has no meaning must drive us to communicate his love. Only through their connection with him will they discover real purpose for their existence and uncover the rich potential he has for their lives.

Spirituality

Many young people are using rave culture to search for a spiritual dimension to life. Dr Russell Newcombe, a Liverpool-based sociologist and researcher, observed that raving can be viewed as a transcendental mind-altering experience that provides psychic relief to 'alienated people in a secular, repressive and materialistic society. Ecstasy and other drugs are the keys that unlock the doors to these desired states of consciousness'. In a high-pressure world, where success is everything and those who are unsuccessful are considered inferior, many are looking for something different. Nicholas Saunders of the *Guardian* surveyed 137 ravers about the effects of Ecstasy on their lives. A significant number reported 'increased spiritual awareness', some adding they 'felt closer to nature, calmer and more appreciative of life itself'.

Young people are not alone in this quest for meaning. People in their twenties, thirties and forties are exploring a growing number of new forms of popular spirituality. This exploration is one of the most significant characteristics of new millennium society. We should not be ashamed, therefore, of talking about spirituality. We must learn to talk about prayer, worship and our sense of God's presence with more conviction and confidence. The apostle Paul demonstrated this confidence when he addressed the council of the city of Athens:

> 'Men of Athens! I see that in every way you are very religious. For as I walked around and looked carefully at your objects of worship, I even found an altar with this inscription: TO AN UNKNOWN GOD. Now what you worship as something unknown I am going to proclaim to you...'

Jesus accepts us as we are. When he comes into our lives, he can make us whole in body, mind and spirit. In Jesus we have a Saviour who gives us a sense of purpose and direction like none other.

Suffering

Even the simplest presentation of the Jesus story will speak into the pain of someone who is hurting emotionally or physically. However, we must also learn how to demonstrate that our faith has helped us in our own difficulties and that knowing Jesus has given us chinks of light in the dark places of our journey through life. When I'm talking to someone recently bereaved, for instance, I often talk about my grief following the death of my mum and how my faith helped me through that. When I'm talking to someone in hospital, I try to draw on my experiences of illness and show how prayer has been a strength and support to me. We can use the experiences in our past to help us relate to the needs of others. Effective Christian witness always takes account of suffering and seeks to apply our personal story to the circumstances of the person we are witnessing to.

Loneliness

Several contemporary research projects support the idea that there is a rising tide of loneliness. I attended a seminar at a national television conference which revealed the findings of research done on the popularity of 'soaps'.

Every week these programmes top the ratings, with shows like *Eastenders*, *Coronation Street* and *Emmerdale* holding audiences of 10–15 million each week. Viewer interaction with the characters featured in the storylines can be astonishing: they may receive hundreds of letters of condolence, birthday cards, even hate-mail each week. Researchers told the conference that the reason for the popularity of such shows is that people are hungry to belong to a community and desperate for relationship. They express these deeply felt needs in their addiction to imaginary worlds and fictional characters. It's a lonely world.

According to sociologist Yvonne Roberts, men are particularly prone to loneliness. In her detailed survey of the conversations of men aged thirty-five, she discovered that while they say a lot, they reveal practically nothing about themselves:

> Men seem to spend a lot of time talking to each other, but very little time actually saying anything which touches on the reality of the lives that they are living ... step outside the formula, and talk about emotions, fear, failure, love, joy – and you become a loner, a bit 'soft' – less of a man.

A man might be facing bankruptcy, terminal cancer or marriage breakdown, but is unlikely to tell his drinking pals anything about it. When asked how he's feeling, he will simply say, 'Everything's fine.' There's plenty of communication but little relationship.

There is loneliness among students, too. Dr Yeap, a lecturer in Instructional Science at the University of Singapore, conducted extensive research among 509 students aged between 13 and 17 years. He concluded that 'adolescent loneliness' was rampant among the sample group, with four out of five students talking freely about their sense of isolation. The statistics show that the loneliness did not diminish if students came from extended families or from wealthier backgrounds. Of the sample group, older teenagers came off worst, with 81% expressing strong feelings of loneliness, even when they lived at home with their parents. One seventeen-year-old wrote, 'How do I get rid of the feeling of emptiness and meaninglessness in my life? I don't think that anyone understands me. How could they, when I don't even understand myself?' This often happens because the family, which should be an enclosure for safety, often becomes an emotional kick-boxing ring. Not only are there insufficient boundaries against external threats, but parents themselves are often the threat!

We live in a society desperate for relationships and our gospel is full of good news about relationships. When we become Christians, we find a new friend in Jesus Christ – someone who loves us, accepts us and remains with us. When we become friends of Jesus, we should discover a whole new friendship network within the life of the church.

The pilgrimage

Christianity isn't a religion designed only to help us at church! It's a faith that brings meaning, strength, direction and healing to the whole of life. It fulfils the needs we have all experienced at one time or another.

I used to believe that there were just two kinds of people, believers and non-believers. After more than fifteen years engaged in front-line evangelism, however, I have to say that I find the process a lot more complicated now than I used to. Many people are making a journey of faith, whether they recognise it or not. They may be at the starting gate or well along the track. If we have a genuine burden for evangelism, we need to discover where they are along the road if we are to move them forward in their faith journey.

One day I challenged my secretary about the amount of

time our staff were giving to the postman who brought the stacks of letters to our office each morning. I was getting irritated by his chit-chat and the evident enthusiasm with which he delivered our post each morning. She drew herself up to her full height and peered at me over the top of her spectacles. 'Recently,' she said, 'you told us that we should be witnesses for Christ where we are. I've got a problem. We're all Christians in this office – who else can I witness to?'

I felt thoroughly and deservedly chastened. Shortly afterwards the postman came in with a terrible confession – he had lost a registered letter. Our office team readily gathered round him, laid hands on his sack and prayed for the lost letter. When he returned the next day, lost letter in hand, we all rejoiced together. Later, when I was preaching to over two thousand people in Westminster Central Hall, I looked across the bright beam of the spotlights and saw the faces of the people in the front row. There, just in front of me, was the postman, smiling in warm affirmation. I believe we helped to move him on in his pilgrimage of faith.

The Engels Scale was devised by missionaries in South America as a means of identifying the process of evangelism. As they researched the response of the people with whom they were working, they discovered that they generally were at ten different levels:

10 Become a Christian
 9 Awareness of personal need
 8 Accept Christian truth
 7 Grasp the truth about Jesus
 6 Investigate Jesus
 5 Interest in Jesus Christ
 4 Contact with Christians
 3 Awareness of Christians
 2 Some awareness of God
 1 No awareness of God

So, some people had no awareness of God at all, had never

sensed his presence and had never believed. Others had some awareness of God, perhaps through aspects of creation such as a sunset or the beauty of the changing seasons. Some knew Christians and a bit about how they live and what they believe. Others had already expressed an interest in Jesus and were fascinated by him as a person.

When I started to use the Englels Scale in my own work, I discovered that it fitted many of the people I was seeking to lead to Christ. I stopped seeing them as just 'believers' or 'non-believers' and began to see them as travellers at different stages of a journey. I began to view them not as 'in' the kingdom of God or 'out' of it, but as 'on the way'. This realisation affected the way I spoke to them and sought to share my faith with them. Some of the detached street kids our teams witness to move from having 'no awareness of God' to 'some awareness of God'. By the end of the week of mission some of them may have had real contact with Christians and have begun to investigate Jesus. One or two may even have travelled as far as becoming Christians themselves.

This kind of thinking has transformed my view of evangelism. I used to try and lead people to Christ in one fell swoop, but now I see evangelism as helping people to take the next step in their journey of faith towards discovering Jesus. Then, one day, they make that discovery. God lives on a bigger map than us and I don't believe he wants the good news about Jesus delivered in such a way that it alienates people and disregards their circumstances. The Lord is working with people before we come on the scene, and he'll be working with them long after we have gone!

Moving people from one to ten on the Engels Scale is the responsibility of the Body of Christ working under his Lordship. God's way is not to ask us to put our foot in a stranger's door to try and move them from points one to ten in 90 seconds! No, if our witness only moved someone one level up the Engel scale, with that witness reinforced by other members of the Body of Christ whom that person met day by day, it would be so much more effective. Thousands would be finding Christ every week and the Body of Christ would be functioning as it was meant to function!

Lifestyle evangelism

Sometimes Jesus called people to leave everything and follow him. In simple obedience, people like Peter, James and John left their boats, their fishing business, their home town, their family and their loved ones to take to the open road with him. But there were others, many others, whom Jesus didn't invite to join him. To them, he simply said, 'Go home.'

The wild Gerasene demoniac, living among the caves and tombs far from civilisation, was considered dangerous and insane. He was chained up but often managed to break free. What a sight he must have been – flowing hair, unkempt beard, wild eyes; blistered and bleeding from the many cuts he'd inflicted on himself. When Jesus healed him, casting a host of demons out of him into a herd of pigs, he was clean, clothed, in his right mind and eager to know what he should do next:

> As Jesus was getting into the boat, the man who had been demon-possessed begged to go with him. Jesus did not let him, but said, 'Go home to your family and tell them how much the Lord has done for you, and how he has had mercy on you.'

When he returned home, that man would have made a profound impression on everyone. The transformation in his life spoke more clearly about the power of Jesus Christ than a thousand articulate sermons. He went home and lived the transformation.

Most of us haven't got quite such a dramatic testimony of the Lord's dealing with us, but who we are and what he has done for us still speak more clearly than anything else. The way we live, the people we are and the priorities we make will all be powerful aspects of our Christian witness to others. This is at the heart of 'lifestyle evangelism'. If there are aspects of our life that the Lord needs to sort out, it's important we allow him to do so.

When Jesus was passing through Jericho, he came across a small man hiding in a tree. Zacchaeus wasn't the most popular guy in town: he worked for the Romans – the enemy – and would have been considered a traitor. Not only that, he was known as a dishonest tax-man and was reputed to be cooking the books. When Jesus visited him and led him to salvation, Zacchaeus didn't leave town to follow Jesus. No! He said, 'Look, Lord! Here and now I give half of my possessions to the poor, and if I have cheated anybody out of anything, I will pay back four times the amount.' We can only begin to imagine the impact such a decision would have made on the small community of Jericho. It would have been the talk of the town! The generosity of the tax-man would have touched the lives of many. Like Zacchaeus, we must learn what it means to witness where we live, in deed as well as in word.

When Jesus met the Samaritan woman by the well, the conversation he had with her left her deeply moved. She raced back to her village and gossiped the good news – 'Come and see the man who told me everything I have ever done!' Through what she said, and the excitement and conviction with which she said it, some believed in Jesus. It's not enough just to share the good news of Jesus through our changed lives and our good deeds. Like the woman, we must 'go home' and tell others. There are opportunities all around us, and daily we should pray for openings to speak about Jesus and tell of what he has done in our lives.

One night I was travelling on a long plane journey with a well-known Christian leader and speaker, Roger Forster. It was a never-ending journey, almost twenty hours in length, and the selection of movies was dire. We couldn't sleep, so we talked and talked. After some considerable time, Roger asked me if I was related to a man called Frost who had once been a London City Missioner around Battersea. I explained that this was my great-grandfather, someone whom I'd never met. Roger told me of the love and grace which shone from this man, and how he'd collected a tribe of children each

Sunday to take to Sunday school. Roger Forster was one of them. I've never met my great-grandfather, but his witness continues through one of my contemporary heroes, Roger Forster.

When you buy a stick of seaside rock, you will often discover that the name of the resort is stamped throughout the whole stick. Break it in the middle, at the end or anywhere else and you will find the name 'Blackpool'. In the same way, our faith must penetrate every aspect of our life – at work, at leisure, in the family and in the community. Lifestyle evangelism is one of the most powerful forms of all Christian witness. As people see our relationship with Christ in the cut and thrust of everyday life, we must pray that they come to understand what he means to us.

Many years ago, I was at a camp for inner city kids. One of the rough, tough lads recommended for the camp was a young teenager called David. One night, beside the dying embers of a camp fire, I overheard one of the leaders, Barrie, ask David if he would like to become a Christian. The young lad nodded affirmatively.

More than twenty years later, I sat in a down-town church in Brixton and joined in one of the most powerful funeral services I've ever been part of. The church was packed to capacity, with chairs down the aisles and the doorways crowded with those who couldn't get in. Soon the coffin was carried into the church. In it was the body of David who had died young of a blood disorder. Barrie from the youth camp was walking slowly behind the coffin as it moved awkwardly down the aisle.

In true Caribbean style, the funeral was relaxed and informal, with laughter, tears and singing. Many people stood up to praise God for David's life and testimony. He had impacted the area in many powerful ways. During his short life, David had accepted the faith, become an ordained minister and lived his witness in one of the most difficult cultural settings for Christian mission. At the end of the service I stood with hundreds of people and watched the cortège drive away. I was moved with emotion. I looked back down the years and remembered how this one life was transformed by Christ and how, in turn, this one life had effected hundreds of other lives. All because Barrie had a burden for evangelism.

Bible references: Ephesians 2:12; Acts 17:22–23; Mark 5:1–20; Luke 19:1–9; John 4:1–42.

Book references: Francis Schaeffer and Everett Koop, *Whatever Happened to the Human Race?*, Marshall, Morgan and Scott, 1980; Erich Fromm, *To have or To Be?*, Cape, 1876; Dr Russell Newcombe, 'Raving and dance drugs and the use of Ecstasy and dance drugs', Liverpool University, 1997; Yvonne Roberts, *Man Enough*, Chatto and Windus, 1984.

Chapter 10

A VISION FOR EVANGELISM

We live in a success-driven society. In practically every profession in recent years there has been a new emphasis on productivity and quality control. In many disciplines the emphasis has been on quantity. How many surgical operations did you perform? How many more insurance policies did you sell this month compared to last? How are your students performing in examinations compared to the national average? This kind of thinking can permeate the life of the church, and especially the field of evangelism. I have known the most credible Christian evangelistic organisations talk about growth targets, new membership indices, 'response' percentages and conversion rates.

When a team of British Methodist ministers recently visited a church in Korea, they were staggered to discover that the church leaders presented a new car each year to 'the most successful soul-winner in the congregation'! Evangelists can easily be seen as the 'sales force' of the church, and programmes of mission and evangelism judged as effective solely by their ability to produce results quickly.

While I have no problem with the concept of effectiveness in mission, or of using our resources in the most productive ways, I don't believe that 'success-driven' evangelism is biblical. Many Christians are discouraged about their witness and feel that they are not 'successful'. I have seen signs of exhaustion in the most keen of evangelical believers. I have met mission-minded Christians who have slogged on, year after year, and grown tired and fed up because of poor results. Their initial enthusiasm has dwindled because of the lack of new converts. I can empathise with these feelings because I have been there myself. I entered the ministry with all the sensitivity of a bull in a china shop! I flew around trying to do everything myself, hoping to bring the world to Christ in a week or two. After a few months I was completely exhausted and somewhat disheartened. One day an older and wiser minister came to see me. He told me that I was trying to do too much, too soon. He showed me that I had been setting targets for myself which were not the Lord's and evangelistic goals that God was not asking me to reach.

The Bible sets out some clear principles for the process of evangelism. If we embark on mission without understanding them, we are likely to end up looking like failed used-car salesmen. Let's look at some of them.

Sow, even when the odds are against you

The task of evangelism can seem pretty hopeless. A witnessing congregation can feel pathetic and outnumbered a thousand to one by those in the local area who have little or no interest in the Christian faith.

One summer I went to help my friend bring in the harvest on his Yorkshire farm. I had no idea what harvesting would be like. As I learned how to drive the tractor, throw bales of straw into the barn and unclog the bailer, I began to realise just how stressful an occupation farming can be. Each night my friend and I would stagger back to the farmhouse covered in sweat and grime, but with a glow of satisfaction that 'all was safely gathered in'.

One day we had to take a trailer full of oil-seed rape from the combine harvester in the field to the large storage silo in the farmyard. I rode through the village on the back of this trailer piled high with shifting seed. I held on to the swaying trailer as we went, but gradually began to sink lower and lower into the cargo until my wellingtons and trousers were filled with the oily black seed and I couldn't move. It was not a pleasant experience! When we arrived at the farmyard, my friend lowered a large black suction pipe into the trailer and watched as the seed was sucked up into the silo. He sighed: 'This stuff is amazing – we sow it in pounds and reap it in tons!' Eventually I was released! As I watched the crop gradually disappearing, I remembered the parable of the mustard seed and understood the full force of its meaning for the first time. In each mustard seed of the gospel there is incalculable potential, and its prospects for growth far exceed our capacity to understand how it happens.

> [Jesus said,] 'The kingdom of heaven is like a mustard seed, which a man took and planted in his field. Though it is the smallest of all your seeds, yet when it grows, it is the largest of garden plants and becomes a tree, so that the birds of the air come and perch in its branches.'

This parable really came alive for me when I visited Gwennap Pit in Cornwall. Every year, thousands of Methodists from around the world visit this large amphitheatre situated miles from anywhere. It is the site where John Wesley used to preach to the Cornish tin miners in the open air, and where hundreds of them found Jesus Christ as Saviour. On one occasion an actor dressed as John Wesley preached in the arena. There were young Methodists from all over the world sitting in the amphitheatre. It was a powerful reminder of Wesley's preaching ministry and of the way the Lord used him to bring revival. As I gazed around at that great crowd, I was overwhelmed by the thought that the preaching of one man could result in a worldwide denomination which currently has a membership of 60 million people. It was a powerful demonstration that the growth potential in any seed of the gospel is greater even than that of a mustard seed!

Our approach to evangelism, therefore, is different from that of a sales force for a new product or an advertising agency selling a new brand. The gospel of Jesus Christ, when faithfully sowed, has its own growth potential. 'Success' and 'sales volume' is not primarily generated by the evangelist – it is inherent in the gospel itself. When just one life is transformed and redeemed by the power of Jesus Christ, that life has the potential to influence thousands more. The gospel is not some inanimate object, like a new car or a soda drink which, once purchased, quickly depreciates or is consumed. No! The Christian message has a power within it which can transform individuals, their families, their communities and their nations. Its effect and influence grow with the years. When we embark on the work of evangelism, we must recognise that every seed of good news we sow has the potential within it to transform not just one life but thousands of lives. Though we sow in pounds, it will eventually be reaped in tons.

Sow, even when you can't see results

We live in a society mesmerised by performance indicators and 'growth graphs', by constant comparisons between sales figures and what they mean in terms of return on investment. The task of evangelism can never be quantified in such terms. The growth of faith is often silent, immeasurable and sometimes seemingly non-existent. Only God knows the final figures, the bottom line. The growth of the Christian church is seldom spectacular. It is often unremarkable, like the new shoot peeping out of the earth. In a society looking for 'quick fix' solutions or the best possible return, the biblical perspective on church growth can seem a bit peculiar!

Several years ago I joined hundreds of other Christians on an Easter Monday pilgrimage organised by the Anglican Diocese of Kent. Hundreds of people walked across the Downs to Canterbury cathedral, following in the footsteps of Augustine of Canterbury, the early Christian missionary, whose monks evangelised England from AD 597. During the service each one of us was given a small unlighted candle. Near the end of the worship the Archbishop lit his candle and explained that this symbolised the light of the gospel which Augustine brought to England. Gradually the flame was passed from candle to candle down the long nave, until thousands of them were all alight.

I was standing at the back of the cathedral during this silent activity, and it was breathtaking to watch. Slowly but surely the light from the candles lit up the dark recesses of the cathedral as it flickered towards me. When the candles were all alight, everyone lifted their candle high and the whole cathedral was a blaze of light. The Archbishop used this as a poignant reminder that the light of the gospel affecting our nation over so many centuries started from such small flickering beginnings. The gospel's growth has been silent, unspectacular, steady; but over the centuries the effect has been staggering. When at last my candle was lit and I passed the flame on, I recognised that I must play my part in the never-ending process of sharing it.

Augustine wasn't the only evangelist of his time. Every year thousands of people from all over the world visit the tiny Scottish island of Iona to thank God for the life and work of an early missionary called Columba. He started to evangelise Scotland with a dozen missionaries from Iona in AD 563. From this base he planted churches all over Scotland. His mission has influenced that country's development ever since. What began as something small has had far-reaching and powerful effects throughout history.

When Robert Raikes was a young man living in eighteenth-century Gloucester, he walked through the town square one Sunday afternoon and saw the children playing on the street. They were illiterate, ill-disciplined and totally outside the life of the church. Raikes despaired of this situation and felt that the future for these children was hopeless. But then he heard a voice saying to him, 'Try, try, try.' He was so convinced that this was a divine commission, he started a Sunday school to help the children read the Bible. Little did he know that what started as a small initiative to reach a handful of youngsters would develop into a worldwide movement touching the lives of millions of young people and bringing countless thousands to Christ. I have attended Sunday schools in prosperous California and in struggling mud-hut villages in Africa. I have spoken at

Sunday schools in Singapore and on banana plantations in the Caribbean. The seed which Raikes sowed has become a harvest.

> 'A man scatters seed on the ground. Night and day, whether he sleeps or gets up, the seed sprouts and grows, though he does not know how. All by itself the soil produces corn – first the stalk, then the ear, then the full grain in the ear. As soon as the grain is ripe, he puts the sickle to it, because the harvest has come.'

For over ten years my wife and I ran youth groups in our home. We had lots of great times. It wasn't all easy, however, and there were some Sunday nights when we used to wonder whether we were wasting our time. At some stage each one of our youth groups had its problems, but one group in south London was a particular pain. Sometimes I felt as if the kids were taking their teenage rebellion out on me rather than their parents! My wife and I came to dread those Sunday evenings. Every suggestion was opposed, every discussion starter ridiculed. There were times when we felt like giving up the group altogether. It constantly baffled us why they kept coming even though they didn't seem to appreciate what was on offer. If the seed was growing we didn't see it, and if our work was bearing fruit we were certainly not aware of it.

One of the most regular attenders at the group was a young black lad called Paul. He sat quietly in the bay window, often smirking in amusement at the antics of the others. Several years later, I met him at a Christian youthwork conference and discovered that he had become a Christian. He was now a full-time youth worker and church leader. He had developed a strong faith and was exercising an important ministry among a very tough group of inner-city kids.

'By the way, Rob,' he whispered. 'Did I ever thank you and Jacqui for running that youth group all those years ago? I don't know where I'd have ended up without it.' Since I had last seen him, smiling as he sat in my lounge all those years ago, the slow but steady growth of the seed had taken place.

Evangelism is often hard, unrewarding and seemingly inef-fective, but whenever we sow the seed we must never under-estimate the growth that can result. The seeds of the gospel grow quietly, invisibly, steadily, but do not be fooled – their growth is for real.

Sow, even when you're feeling a failure

We live in a success-orientated society, in which the 'sales-man of the year' is rewarded with fine holidays or honoured at expensive banquets. In some churches in the United States there is a similar culture in evangelism, with prestigious awards for the 'evangelist of the year' and accolades for those considered to be best at spreading the gospel. I do not find a biblical foundation for such practices, and I believe that Jesus Christ should always remain the centre of our focus as the one who receives all the glory. In his letter to the church in Corinth, the apostle Paul wrote:

> The Lord has assigned to each his task. I planted the seed, Apollos watered it, but God made it grow. So neither he who plants nor he who waters is anything, but only God, who makes things grow.

I once met a young Indian Christian called Augustine. Some years ago he had a dream in which the Lord called him to give up everything and travel to northern India to plant some new churches. In simple obedience he sold his home, left his job and moved to northern India with his family. He could not interest any missionary societies in his vision, but at last two elderly ladies working for the Elim Church decided to support him. They had worked in the area for many years and had found the people hard and unresponsive. These two missionaries offered hospitality and support to Augustine and his family in the early days of his ministry. Eventually, however, their term of service was over and they came back to England. It was a sad departure, because their combined work had shown no tangible results.

Augustine continued the work where they left off and at last some hardened criminals in a local jail were converted by Christ. Such was the effect of these conversions on the community that many others came to follow Christ. Augustine was able to start a church, and he took teams from this new congregation to evangelise the area. Soon their work led to church groups springing up in many villages around the region. There was still great opposition, but many came to know Jesus Christ as Lord and Saviour.

I first met Augustine when I was visiting the British Elim Church's annual conference in Bognor Regis. He was standing at the lectern in the conference hall and speaking to hundreds of British pastors and church leaders. In his speech Augustine paid tribute to the faithfulness in prayer and evangelism of those two elderly missionaries, and told everyone that it was they who had sown the seed for the harvest he had reaped. At the same meeting Augustine handed over the title deeds of the twenty churches to the Elim denomination, in recognition of the faithful work of those two missionaries. Their seeming 'failure' in evangelism had in fact been the preparation work for Augustine's 'success'.

We may like to try and measure our effectiveness in evangelism, but it's a fool's game. God, and God alone, brings the increase. When we sow the seed of the gospel, we may never know what harvest will one day be reaped. We are called to be faithful rather than successful. From time to time the Lord does give us a glimpse of the harvest, however, and it can come as a real surprise. One night in Salford when I was on the road with an evangelistic presentation called 'Travelling Workshop', my car was broken into and my case stolen. I had to borrow clothes for the next stage of the tour. I felt thoroughly fed up. As my team and I set out for Hull the next morning, it was snowing heavily and the M62 was like a skating rink. The thick snow piled onto the windscreen and the car engine laboured as we motored on through the deepening slush. The three of us who were travelling all had streaming colds and, as a team, we were at an all-time low.

Eventually we found the church where we were to present our evangelistic production. A small audience of thirty arrived and stamped their snowy feet in the hallway, making the entrance dangerously slippery. In the corridor which was our make-shift dressing room, we all groaned. The whole enterprise seemed pointless! We had made a hazardous journey, and for what? Thirty people who gave the distinct impression they wanted our production to finish as soon as possible since the weather was getting worse. So we cut the presentation short and went to our accommodation feeling rather the worse for wear. There had been no response to the evangelistic challenge, and the whole exhausting enterprise seemed like a total waste of effort.

Several years later, when I was speaking at a large student conference in Newcastle, a young woman came up to me and beamed. 'You won't recognise me, but I gave my life to the Lord one night in a blizzard in Hull. Everything's been different since then. I never answered the appeal, but that was the night when I first met Jesus.'

My team and I had felt like pathetic failures that night in Hull. Everything was against us and the work of evangelism seemed a sheer waste. But God had other plans. He took the seed we sowed and brought a wonderful increase. To God be the glory, because he did it – not us!

Sow, even when the soil seems hard

When there was nothing to see but bare fields and barren land, Jesus declared, 'I tell you, open your eyes and look at the fields! They are ripe for harvest.' He was looking with the eye of faith. He could see the crop yet to grow, the bountiful harvest yet to be. He could see the distant future, the sower and the reaper rejoicing together. The field may look barren, but as long as the seed is scattered there is enormous potential for harvest. The one who sows is called not to be successful, only faithful; not to imagine what might have been, only what will surely be; not to make gloomy predictions about the outcome, only to sow in hope. The sower should never feel despondent, for, in the providence of God, he or she will surely reap a result.

Sowing has been out of fashion for too long. Those who should have scattered the seed have looked at the barren fields and decided to stay at home. We need the Holy Spirit to give us a new vision for reaching people in the most unlikely situations. But vision doesn't grow through policy meetings; it is something God gives to us as we wait on him and seek his holy will. Jesus commissioned us to go 'into all the world', but he didn't expect us only to sow the seed in what we might consider fertile situations. We are called to sow even in the hard places, not just where we consider that 'the grass grows greener'.

In 1865 no-one would have viewed the East End of London as a potential harvest for the kingdom of God. One night that year, however, William Booth was walking home down the Commercial Road when he became overwhelmed by the needs of the people. When he got home he told his wife, 'As I passed by the doors of those gin palaces tonight I seemed to hear a voice saying, "Where can you find such heathen as these, and where is there so great a need for your labours?" I felt as though I ought at all costs to stop and preach to those East End multitudes.'

Booth was a powerful evangelist and a well-known leader in the Methodist Church. Yet he turned his back on it all to respond to the call to go to a 'barren land'. Booth sowed seeds of the gospel in the East End which bore a harvest throughout the world through the ministry of the Salvation Army. Who would have imagined that such a place could have produced a movement of such fervour and compassion.

When I first became a minister, I was inundated with young couples who wanted to get married in the church. The chapel had a very traditional exterior with a tall spire and a pretty garden which people liked 'for the photos'. So the church tended to attract wedding couples for all the wrong reasons. Each week I held wedding interviews and would see three couples in an evening, spending up to an hour with each. During the months before the wedding, I tried to give each couple three interviews in order to get to know them well. The first meeting was very much an introductory session, in which I established a relationship and discussed their plans. The final interview dealt with practical arrangements, and we would 'talk through' the service together. But the second interview was always the most crucial. During this session, I tried to convey something of how faith in Jesus Christ could strengthen and sustain their life together. I hoped that through this some of them might find a faith right at the start of their married life together.

This second interview was always tricky. Sometimes the couple would try to steer the conversation away from anything spiritual and divert the flow to subjects they found more approachable. I often found these marriage preparation talks deeply discouraging. The whole enterprise seemed like 'barren land'. One couple, however, didn't try to steer the conversation away from the Lord but wanted to know more. They came from outside the life of the church, but they returned again and again to find out more about Jesus. Eventually they gave their lives to Christ. A few years ago I stood in their Yorkshire manse and marvelled at what the Lord had done. Here they were, years later, at the start of their own ministry for Christ. I found it a very emotional experience to talk with them and to hear how they too witness to the couples who come to get married in their church.

We must never write off any soil as 'barren'. It is our task to sow the seed, not predict the outcome. Church history indicates that evangelism in the unlikeliest places and among the most resistant of peoples can bring the biggest harvest of all!

Sow, even when the task seems daunting

A harvest vision sees the gospel as a mustard seed whose growth potential is beyond belief. It sees the gospel as a seed growing silently whose progress cannot be truly measured. It sees the gospel as a seed which, even when planted in the most barren place, can become a mighty harvest. Perhaps the most famous of Jesus' parables is the story of the sower and the seed:

> 'A farmer went out to sow his seed. As he was scattering the seed, some fell along the path, and the birds came and ate it up. Some fell on rocky places, where it did not have much soil. It sprang up quickly, because the soil was shallow. But when the sun came up, the plants were scorched, and they withered because they had no root. Other seed fell among thorns, which grew up and choked the plants, so that they did not bear grain. Still other seed fell on good soil. It came up, grew and produced a crop, multiplying thirty, sixty, or even a hundred times.'

Please note that the story doesn't say, 'A farmer went out to sow, but first he did a statistical return on the prospects of harvest.' Or, 'a farmer went out to sow, but first he did a public opinion poll on the political correctness of such an activity.' Or, 'a farmer went out to sow, but first called a committee together to see if they'd give him permission to do so.' No! *A sower went out to sow.*

If you want a good harvest, don't let a statistician sow the seed. He will stand in the autumn furrow and try to calculate the chances of the seed surviving. He will anticipate chill winds, heavy snows and frozen earth, and forecast a poor harvest if any at all. As the writer of Ecclesiastes observed, 'Whoever watches the wind will not plant; whoever looks at the clouds will not reap.'

If you want a good harvest, don't use a pollster to sow the seed. He will stand, opinion poll in one hand and calculator in the other, and compute the chances of a crop. He has canvassed public opinion and decided that harvests aren't popular any more. He has examined the complex food-markets of the world and concluded there's insufficient demand. So he recommends that the harvest be cancelled this year.

If you want a good harvest, don't ask a committee to sow the seed. They will stand at the edge of the field muttering disapprovingly to each other and protecting their pristine green wellingtons from the mud. Committees cannot sow without a majority and, as they rarely agree on anything, majorities are hard to find. They will conclude that the soil is poor and the prospects bleak. Perhaps next year...

If you want a good harvest, don't employ an agricultural expert to sow the seed. His diploma in soil management, degree in farm technology and doctorate in agrarian history have not prepared him for such a task. He sits at his computer and produces colour graphs projecting the failure of the crop, but he never sows seed himself. He never ventures out into the field or feels the rich dark soil running through his fingers. His thesis argues that harvests are a thing of the past. Sowing of seed is no longer worth the effort.

But somewhere beyond the grey boundaries of the urban sprawl, a sower goes out to sow. He barely understands the process, let alone the depressing theoretical predictions of the experts. He throws the raw seed into the gusting wind and his heart is full of hope. He is driven by a conviction too deep for words and he knows that, against all odds, the harvest will surely come.

Sowing must be done by those who are committed to the task and who know that, out of the faithfulness of their evangelism, the harvest will come. Sadly, 'the harvest is plentiful but the workers are few.' Pray that the Lord of the harvest will send out others to join in this work. Pray that he will open the eyes of many in our churches today to see this vision and to know the privilege and joy of becoming sowers of the seed.

Bible references: Matthew 13:31–32; Mark 4:26–29; 1 Corinthians 3:5–7; John 4:35; Mark 4:3–8; Ecclesiastes 11:4; Matthew 9:37.

AN AUDIT OF CHURCH LIFE

1. What kind of church do we represent? How many hold church membership? What is our average congregation in the morning, in the evening? What mid-week meetings are there, if any? Are they mainly inward-focused or outward-focused? Do we have a Sunday school or other children's groups? Is there a women's fellowship? Are there any house groups? What is the average age of the congregation? Do we have any young families? Have we received any new members in recent months?

2. In what ways does our church interface with the local community? How do we view ourselves? Do we feel we have we become a clique? How do others see us? Do we regularly bring friends and colleagues to see what's happening? Are there regular 'ways in' to the church (eg special 'guest events')? Are there opportunities for people to hear about Jesus and respond to him? Are there natural ways to follow up those who come to faith? Have there been any new converts recently? Are there new signs of faith and witness? Are our members effective witnesses? Do we provide training in evangelism and witness? Do we have a vision for growth? Does our church function more for its members or for those outside the life of the church? Are we welcoming and friendly?

3. What kind of area are we working in? Do many people commute? What industry are most people in the area involved in? Are there many retired folk? Are there many teenagers or children in the area? Are there belts of new housing? What significant changes, if any, are happening to the character and constituency of people in our catchment area? Have people moved into the congregation as newcomers to the area? If not, why not?

4. What kind of mission outreach are other churches doing nearby? Should we be working with them? How can we be partners in mission yet avoid competition? What kind of ecumenical relationships do we have? Is there a church from a different denomination nearby? Do we have united services with another church regularly, occasionally, never? Would it be good for the mission to be an ecumenical venture? Is the vicar/minister supportive of our work?

5. How have things been going recently? Has our youthwork grown or declined? Have we had an influx of new children in the Sunday school? Are we particularly concerned about the numbers of ageing church members? Are some of our stalwarts moving away? Have any groups or organisations in the church recently closed down, opened up? How is the spiritual life of the church? Is there any need for the renewal of our prayer life? Have there been any evangelistic outreach activities in recent years? Are there any particular things within the life of our church that we are excited about?

6. How do we think the visiting mission team could help us in the ongoing life and witness of our church? Should we restart or strengthen the children's work, start a youth fellowship, visit people in the area, make contact with local schools, train new leaders in evangelism, share in encouraging the prayer life of church members, make contact with people on the community roll, attempt to reach those outside the orbit of the church, make contact with those who have recently moved into the community?

7. In what ways do we think our church could prepare for a mission team (eg prepare a list of people for making visits, organise 'entry' to local schools)? What kind of facilities do we have in the church (eg a flush toilet, a kitchen)? How many rooms are there? Can local hospitality or sleeping accommodation be offered to the visiting mission team? Can we offer camp beds, help with catering?

8. In what ways could the church follow up the work of the mission (eg form a nurture group for new converts, provide teachers for a new Sunday school or children's group, continue running a new prayer group or house group)?

Appendix 2

A SAMPLE COMMUNITY SURVEY

Age? Sex? Occupation?
Do you work locally?
How long have you lived in the area?
Do you talk to your neighbours, or visit them?
What sort of neighbourhood is this? How would you describe it?
What are the main problems in this area?
What facilities are lacking in this area?
To whom would you look to help you in a time of crisis?
Where would you recommend people go if they want to meet new
friends, get help or advice, have a good time?
Do you belong to any groups in this area?
Where do you meet people socially around here?
Do you attend church?
Do you know anyone who does?
What is your image of the local churches?
What would you like to see the churches doing in this area?

Appendix 3

SOME EXAMPLES OF AIMS AND GOALS FOR LOCAL MISSION

Contact new families who have moved into the area, and spend
time with them.
Start, or work with, a mother-and-baby group.
Work in local schools with the aim of strengthening the church's
youth programme.
Start a series of house groups or Alpha groups.
Contact lapsed church members.
Spend time with the elderly, the housebound and the sick.
Work with the unemployed or other groups who may feel alien-
ated from the community.

Appendix 4

PREPARING A CHURCH VISION STATEMENT

A church may wish to use the following agenda after the completion of the community survey. It is designed to move the church towards creating its own vision statement.

1. What new opportunities for witness have we identified within our community? What new people-groups have we found?

2. What local needs have we found and how can we meet them?

3. Do we need to relocate our work to where the people are?

4. Do we need to develop forms of worship that are more culturally relevant to the groups identified?

5. What is our strategy for evangelism in our area?

6. How can we make initial contact with the target community?

7. How can we engage people in that group in a serious consideration of Christian faith?

8. How can we encourage a firm commitment to Christ and disciple new converts?

9. Should we begin public worship in this newly identified area and, if so, how can we train up new local leaders?

10. Do we need to become more 'down-market' and approachable?

11. Do we believe God has a future for our church?

Appendix 5

PROGRAMME FOR A WEEK OF MISSION

First Saturday
Group A and Group B

1.00	Visiting team arrives at central venue for registration, orientation and training.
2.00	Celebration.
4.00	Team is taken by hosts to the church.
6.00	Private team-time for getting to know each other and for organising team's input into the evening's welcome session.
8.00	Team is welcomed by the church, with a time of sharing, coffee and informal 'getting to know you'.
10.00	Short planning session for Sunday's services. NB These services do not have to be dance/music extravaganzas! Team involvement would involve simply doing the Bible reading, giving a testimony and providing a leader to preach.
11.00	Brief epilogue and bed.

Sunday
Group A and Group B

7.45	Team quiet time, for personal devotions.
8.00	Breakfast.
10.00	Morning service at the church's normal time, with the team leader preaching. This should be aimed at the local church and families. A good time for visiting team to meet the whole church.
1.00	Members of the team have lunch in local homes.
3.00	Sports afternoon in a park, beach or garden (in the church hall if wet). This is a time for the whole church family. Games could be organised by the team and the church.
5.00	Picnic tea.
6.00	Open-air witness at the picnic site, with team leader preaching. Alternatively, everyone could go back to the church for the regular evening service. Possibly other churches in the area could be invited to take part.

8.30	Divide into Groups A and B for preparation and planning. Team pastor interviews each team member. Also allow opportunity for people to give gifts and share testimonies.
10.00	Brief epilogue and bed.

Monday

	Group A	Group B
7.45	Quiet time.	
8.00	Team breakfast.	
9.30	Travel to regional training centre.	'Thought for the Day': team invites the church to join them for Bible study and prayer.
10.00	Regional training, fellowship and feedback. Local youth invited to join in.	
10.30	Neighbourhood prayer walk with members of the church.	
12.30	Travel back to team base.	
1.00	Lunch – hot meal provided by the church, to be eaten privately as a team.	
2.30	Random acts of kindness, eg free car-wash, great pen give-away, neighbourhood task force, visiting the sick and housebound.	Door-knocking: 'We are local Christians and we are having a special day of prayer. Have you any needs you would like us to pray for?'
4.30	Free time, rest and showers.	
6.00	Sausage Sizzle: barbecue for Groups A and B and local young people (11–13s), leading into a water fight for local people and Group A.	
7.30	Fellowship, church prayer vigil, then coffee for the team, the church and others visiting from the area.	
9.00	Detached youthwork, eg talking to young people on the street, bringing them back to the church hall for 'chip parties' or 'Coke and conversation'. Alternatively, church-based youthwork.	Free time.
10.30	Team debrief.	
11.00	End.	

Tuesday

	Group A	Group B
7.30	Men's Breakfast (cooked!) with some Christian input from the visiting team.	
9.30	'Thought for the Day': team invites the church to join them for Bible study and prayer.	
10.30	J Club: games, quizzes, competitions, etc, for 6–9s. Aims to explore the story of Jesus and encourage children to follow him; led by the team.	Preparation for street theatre, eg making signs/signboards, dressing up as clowns. Also preparation for the cream tea.
12.30	Sandwich lunch.	
1.00	Provides support for Group B with the street theatre by giving out tracts, etc.	Open-air street theatre.
2.30	Quiet time.	Free time.
3.30	English cream tea, served in the homes and gardens of church members.	
6.00	Hot meal provided by the church.	
7.00	Preparation for J Club and the sleepover event.	Preparation for pub outreach.
8.00	Detached youthwork (see Monday 9.00pm).	Outreach in pubs and possibly discussion groups in side rooms.
10.30	Team debrief and prayer: discussing people and situations encountered during the day, and planning the team's programme for the following day.	
11.00	End.	

Wednesday

	Group A	Group B
7.45	Quiet time.	
8.00	Breakfast.	
9.30	'Thought for the Day'.	
10.30	J Club (see Tuesday 10.30am).	Coffee morning, showing video on parenting; either in the church hall or in

10.30	J Club continued.	someone's home; led by the team with local folk participating.
12.00	J Club children perform their favourite songs for parents.	
1.00	Lunch provided by church.	
2.30	Preparation for Thursday's J Club.	Devotional meeting in church for older members and their friends.
3.30	Free afternoon, with both groups together.	
5.00	Evening meal.	
6.30	Transport to district adult celebration.	
7.00	Youth pizza parties, or 'cake and Mars Bars' parties; in private homes.	District adult celebration. Group B and adults from local churches gather together for a large, lively celebration with art and music. Encourage all churches to bring a coach-load to this event.
9.30	Transport back to team base.	
10.30	Detached youthwork, possibly leading to a sleepover for church-affiliated young people on church premises.	Free time
11.00	Epilogue and bed.	

Thursday

	Group A	*Group B*
7.45	Quiet time.	
8.00	Breakfast.	
9.30	'Thought for the Day'.	
10.30	J Club.	Coffee morning in a local hotel, restaurant or pub (must be a non-church venue), aimed at women. Outreach/evangelistic talk by guest speaker.
1.00	Hot meal provided by church.	
2.30	Preparation for	Visiting the housebound.

	Friday's J Club.	Invite local people to accompany the team on these visits.
3.30	Door-knocking to specified homes, ie warm contacts selected by church.	
4.30	Free time.	
5.30	Sandwiches provided by church.	
7.00	Team and local young people transported to youth culture celebration held locally.	Preparation for neighbourhood groups.
7.30	Youth culture celebration.	Neighbourhood groups: house groups, neighbours groups, coffee evenings, cheese-and-wine parties. These provide opportunities for the team to share in testimony and engage in conversation with local people.
10.30	Team debrief.	
11.00	Epilogue and bed.	

Friday
Group A and Group B

7.45	Quiet time.
8.00	Breakfast.
9.30	'Thought for the Day'.
10.30	J Club: Open to all the family for the whole morning; led as an 'all-age' worship, with a challenge at the end.
1.00	Sandwich meal provided by the church, during which the team meets with the minister and other church leaders for feedback on mission.
1.20	Follow-up of various contacts made throughout the week.
2.00	Between now and 7.30 pm, team pastor meets with individual team members for mission debriefing, to complete individual team member's report to take back to their home minister. Each interview should close with prayer.

3.00	Informal preparations for the evening's community celebrations.
5.00	Hot meal provided by the church.
7.30	Time of prayer for evening celebration.
8.00	Community celebration, including music, drama and testimony, from both local people and visiting team. Proclamation of the gospel. The evening ends with coffee and cake.
10.00	Clearing up.
11.00	Debrief, epilogue and bed.

Final Saturday
Group A and Group B

7.45	Quiet time.
8.00	Breakfast.
Morning	Church transports visiting team to central location, for team debriefing.
Afternoon	Team members travel home.